THE ADVOCATE

THE ADVOCATE

The Spirit of Truth
in the Life of the Individual Christian

Andrew Apostoli, C.F.R.

Foreword by
Alan Napleton

TAN Books
Charlotte, North Carolina

Permission for the release of these three titles under the auspices of TAN Books has been granted by the Society of St. Paul, Inc., ST PAULS / Alba House, 2187 Victory Blvd., Staten Island, NY., USA.

In composing this work, Father Apostoli relied principally on his vast store of knowledge for biblical quotations and, as such, many passages may be paraphrased or seem to derive from a number of different authorized Catholic versions of the Bible.

Cover and interior design by Caroline Kiser

Images by Nancy Bauer and Sopelkin / Shutterstock

ISBN: 978-1-5051-1045-6

Published in the United States by
TAN Books
PO Box 410487
Charlotte, North Carolina 28241
www.TANBooks.com

Printed and bound in the United States of America

DEDICATION

With filial love and devotion,
the original version of this book
was dedicated to the Blessed Virgin Mary, who,
as the chosen Daughter of the Eternal Father,
conceived in her womb Jesus Christ,
"the Way, the Truth and the Life"
through the overshadowing of the Holy Spirit
that He might be proclaimed to the whole world,

and

to Pope St. John Paul II,
whose wholehearted fidelity to Jesus Christ
made him a courageous prophet of the Most High
and a faithful evangelist of the splendor of truth!

* * * * *

This present revised edition of the book is also dedicated
to Pope Emeritus Benedict XVI,
who constantly warned us of the "tyranny of relativism"
and to Pope Francis,
who has called us to be missionaries of the truth.

TABLE OF CONTENTS

ACKNOWLEDGMENTS

THIS BOOK IS TRULY the fruit of dedication on the part of certain individuals. Without their help, it would never have been completed. I first wish to thank Mary Majkowski, who so kindly and patiently typed and retyped the original contents through many revisions. Without her tremendous contribution of time, effort, and materials, as well as her encouragement, I do not believe this book would have ever come to press. I also want to thank her husband Edward and her family with whom I shared many meals as Mary and I worked on the book. I also wish to thank Renee Bumb Smith for her help in organizing and then editing the text. I am grateful to her husband Kevin for his support as well.

I wish also to acknowledge the many people who have supported the writing of this book with their prayers and encouragement over the period of its preparation. If it pleases God, may the many prayers offered for its completion obtain special graces for those who read it!

The author also wishes to thank Alba House for graciously agreeing to publish the first edition of this book and TAN Books for publishing this second edition.

For this second edition, the author wishes to thank Pam Presbitero for her help with researching the various quotes and prayers that have been added to this work, as well as editing and proofing the manuscript. The author also wishes to thank Alan Napleton from the Catholic Marketing Network and Conor Gallagher of TAN Books for agreeing to reprint this updated version.

No acknowledgment would be complete without thanking Almighty God for the grace to complete this work. It was written in honor of the Blessed Trinity, to give praise and glory to the Father, the Son, and the Holy Spirit, Who live and reign, the same yesterday, today, and forever!

The author would like to thank in a very special way Our Blessed Mother, whose constant intercession was sought throughout the writing of this book. Finally, I wish to thank one of the newest Doctors of the Church, St. Thérèse of Lisieux, for her spiritual encouragement in the writing of this book.

Foreword to the
Golden Jubilee Edition

SOONER OR LATER, I think we all come to realize that we are on a journey, a realization that often comes with age as we are faced with the certainty of our own death and begin to contemplate what's next. Certainly, the individual life journeys of each of us are different, faced as we are with an endless option of paths and choices. But even with all the variety of options and challenges that we encounter, our journeys are still somehow similar in that we were created to end up in the same place—in the arms of a loving God. Whether we believe it or not, that is our true destiny.

Like each of you, my journey has been unique. I've experienced more than my fair share of joy, and I am no stranger to the pain and suffering that we all inevitably confront along the way. Now that I'm in my late 60s, I look back and realize that the decisive moment in my journey took place nearly thirty years ago, when I made the decision to leave the corporate world and offer to God whatever modest talents I possessed for the work of His Church.

Not surprisingly, this course of action does not usually reward one with earthly treasure. However, it often provides one with riches of a more enduring kind, and sometimes allows you the company of some of the most exceptional people on the face of the earth. People who have made the conscious decision to serve their Creator completely, giving Him their all, and leaving nothing for themselves. People who radiate love so clearly, yet powerfully, that they truly reflect Christ's love for us and, like Christ, inexplicably draw us to them and him. Father Andrew Apostoli, CFR is one such soul. I have come to know him as a wise and holy man of God who has fully dedicated his life to his vocation as a Franciscan friar for over fifty years. I feel very privileged and blessed that he has played such an important role in my journey!

I have known Father Andrew for nearly thirty years, and his friendship and spiritual guidance has meant more to me than I think he will ever know. When we first met, I had just experienced a reawakening to my Catholic faith and found myself coordinating a conference at a place that we have both come to love, a shrine in the heart of Mexico City that marks the spot where the Queen of Heaven appeared to a humble indigenous man nearly 500 years ago—the Shrine of Our Lady of Guadalupe. Here, the Mother of God spoke of her love and help that was available to each of us. In this Shrine, she left an image of herself on St. Juan Diego's tilma, which has been miraculously preserved for nearly five centuries.

Father Andrew spoke at that conference, and that very same day we became fast and dear friends. We decided then and there to make an annual pilgrimage to Our Lady's Shrine and did so for over a decade, bringing along hundreds of other individuals and families from all over the country.

Father Andrew's love for our heavenly Mother was apparent even then, and it was truly a beautiful thing to behold. His deep devotion to Our Lady, which was so apparent as I watched him speak about her on those trips, shines through in his many conferences, TV and radio appearances, and writings.

I have also spent a lot of time with Father Andrew in Yonkers, at his New York Friary in the heart of the Bronx. While there I have observed the way in which the younger men and women in this growing religious order look up to him as a spiritual father. With great admiration and respect, they lovingly seek his guidance, deriving benefit from, as have so many others, his deep store of spiritual and practical wisdom. Father has also taken me to some of the mission outlets run by the CFR's, places where I think he feels most at home. There, alongside the men and women of his community, he joyfully tends to the needs of God's poor and neglected; such missions are oases in the middle of the concrete jungle, places where people are reminded that they, too, are children of God.

Although Father Andrew is always very busy serving the Lord, he has never refused any request that I have made of him. Almost twenty years ago, I asked if he would serve as spiritual director for a new organization I had founded, and, of course, he agreed. Called the Catholic Marketing Network, this apostolate is made up of a variety of individuals and entities serving the Lord in many ways. Since the organization was comprised mostly of lay people who had certain temporal responsibilities that went along with their spiritual activities, I asked Father to help the organization navigate through the often unusual, challenging, and overlapping worlds of spirituality and commerce. Keeping the spiritual element at the fore, Father Andrew helped to create a Eucharist-centered organization while making himself available to the many individuals who have gotten to know and love him as their spiritual guide and mentor in the effort to bring quality Catholic products to God's people.

Father Andrew was greatly blessed in that he was ordained to the priesthood by the late great Archbishop Fulton J. Sheen. And quite providentially, Father was to play a pivotal role in the effort to open the cause for this wonderful churchman's canonization. After several years of petitioning numerous dioceses to open the cause, Bishop Daniel R. Jenky, C.S.C. of the Diocese of Peoria agreed to do so. As soon as it was open, Father asked me to help organize the Archbishop Fulton J. Sheen Foundation and serve as its founding Executive Director. I was amazed and humbled that someone like me would be given the privilege to serve in such an important role. We worked very closely together for several years, raising money to help cover the necessary costs associated with the cause, while encouraging prayers that the good Archbishop might someday be officially declared a saint of the Catholic Church. Father is a staunch devotee of Archbishop Sheen and quotes him often in his own talks and writings, thus leading others, like myself, to an increased appreciation for and devotion to the great man. I am truly amazed by the clarity and moral force of his teachings, which have greatly edified me in my own spiritual journey. Sheen's influence on my life I owe to Father Andrew.

It is said that you can learn a lot about the founder of a religious order by observing the present-day behavior of its members. Certainly, St. Francis is one of the Church's most popular saints, loved all over the world by both Catholics and non-Catholics alike. His simplicity, humility, and desire to give God his all made him a true model of Christian discipleship. Seeking to follow the example of this great saint, who sought to imitate Our Lord and Savior, is a noble and mighty goal, and, in human terms, may seem unattainable. But one need only look to the Franciscan Friars of the Renewal to see such an imitation of Francis' imitation of Christ lived out so beautifully. As a co-founder of this religious order, Father Andrew's life truly exemplifies the Christian values of total service and generous giving that are the hallmarks of the spirit of St. Francis.

On the day of his ordination, then Bishop Fulton Sheen asked Father Andrew whether he had been given much instruction on the Holy Spirit during his time in the seminary. Responding that he had not, Bishop Sheen encouraged the newly ordained priest to study, preach, and teach on the Third Person of the Holy Trinity, Whom he referred to at the time as "The Forgotten God." Father Andrew took this advice to heart. Today, he is a powerful and effective teacher on the Holy Spirit. These instructional and insightful books on the Spirit of God are priceless in their depth of understanding and elucidation of the Third Person of the Holy Trinity of Whom Christ Himself said, ". . . he will teach you all things and bring to your remembrance all that I have said to you" (Jn 14:26). It is the Holy Spirit—the Paraclete,

Comforter, and Advocate—Who explains and reveals to hurting mankind the mind and love of God.

It is fitting that these three books on the Holy Spirit have been updated for re-release this year in which Father Andrew marks his 50th anniversary as a priest. A true man of God, he has heroically lived out his calling to be an Alter Christus, another Christ, who has helped this poor soul and so many others on the journey that will end, God willing, in the arms of our loving God.

Alan Napleton
President, Catholic Marketing Network
Fort Worth, TX
January 2017

Author's Preface

THIS IS MY THIRD BOOK on the Holy Spirit. Because its theme is truth, it may well be the most important. This book definitely has the distinction of being the longest in preparation. As I was writing at intervals in between other duties and preoccupations, the topic area of the Holy Spirit and truth kept expanding. I am grateful to God that I was able to finish it initially during the year 1998, the year Pope (St.) John Paul II dedicated to the Holy Spirit.

The material in this present book focuses on the role of the Spirit of Truth working in the life of the individual Christian. Another of my books on the Holy Spirit focuses on the Spirit of Truth at work in the community of the Church. This is a very important topic area. We are experiencing in today's society a real crisis in regard to truth. Truth, along with other closely associated moral values such as justice, honesty, integrity, and respect, is being rejected in our post-Christian, secular humanist culture. It is being distorted, perverted, and even outrightly denied.

In the struggle to reestablish the essential value of truth in our present society, we know we cannot succeed without help from our Lord, Jesus Christ, Who called Himself "the

Truth" (cf. John 14:6). It is He Who promised to send us the Advocate, the Spirit of Truth, from the Father to "lead us into all truth" (cf. John 16:13) and to "prove the world wrong" (cf. John 16:8) regarding its refusal to believe in Jesus as the Son of God and only Savior, as well as its many false moral values. It is my hope that this book will enlighten all who read it in regard to the wonderful role of the Spirit of Truth in our daily lives. May it also inspire its readers to have a greater personal devotion to the Third Divine Person of the Blessed Trinity and a greater confidence in His constant presence and working in our lives.

Come, Advocate, Spirit of Truth,
and fill the hearts of Your faithful
with the Light of Your Truth
and the Fire of Your Love!

Fr. Andrew Apostoli, CFR
St. Leopold Friary
Yonkers, New York
May 15, 2016
Pentecost Sunday

INTRODUCTION
How Do People Look at "Truth" Today?

UNFORTUNATELY, MANY PEOPLE TODAY are not inclined to read a book on truth. The reason is simple: unlike just a generation ago, truth no longer has a place of prominence in our contemporary society. In the not-so-distant past, people generally looked upon truth as a stable and necessary value. It was something objective and enduring, and not subject to public opinion. People accepted the truth and based their lives upon it. They guided their daily actions by the truths they believed in. And when it came to the truth about God, especially about His existence and His revelation to us, many people were ready to lay down their lives for it.[1]

---

1 These men and women were called "martyrs," from the Greek word meaning "witness." These martyrs were considered "witnesses" to the supreme truths about God and His plan for us.

Secular Society Has Devalued "Truth"

Much of this has changed in our contemporary secular society. Today, the very idea of truth is unclear, uncertain, even elusive. For many, truth is simply whatever a person chooses it to be. This is why so many today cut corners on issues of truth.

When it comes to believing the truth, for example, many consult the latest opinion poll, or the current "ratings" on a given idea, much as if they were consulting the results of a "popularity contest."

Little or no consideration is given as to whether the values or statements in question are objectively true or false, or whether they will stand the test of time because they possess something enduring and are not just a passing fad. Many people today accept as "truths" beliefs that are simply nothing more than empty rhetoric and false promises, or simply illusory hopes and wishful thinking. From an objective reality, truth has become purely subjective: "truth" is whatever a person wants it to be! This is the "tyranny of relativism" that Pope Benedict XVI often warned against.

In a similar way, when it comes to living by values that are "true"—real and genuine rather than false or empty—people today often look at what others are doing and simply imitate them. In this way, they are content to "keep up with the Joneses." They readily follow the simplest and easiest solution (what might be called the "quick fix" approach), regardless of whether it is morally right or wrong, or whether it adversely affects others or not.

To sum up, in today's society, dominated as it is by the secular humanist's values and behavior patterns, what matters for many people in their beliefs and daily living is "what works" (translation: achieves the desired effect, regardless of its consequences for themselves or others), what is "most expedient" (translation: the quickest and easiest possible solution), or what can be labeled as "politically correct" (translation: allows them to go along with the crowd and not feel uncomfortable or encounter any unpleasant criticism).

The Christian's Attitude toward Truth

The Christian's attitude toward truth—both in believing it and living it—stands in sharp contrast to the secular humanist's attitude. The Christian asks: "What did God reveal? What does the Church teach?" In contrast, the secular humanist asks: "What do I want to think is true? How do I feel about a certain statement or value?" The Christian is a man or woman willing to adjust his or her personal choice to the truth. In contrast, the secular humanist is a man or woman ready to adjust truth to his or her personal choice.

Facing the Present "Crisis of Truth"

There is indeed a real crisis of truth in the world today! What has caused this crisis of truth? How can it be resolved'? These are critical questions that we shall try to answer in the light of God's revelation. We shall first look at the roots of this crisis of truth. We shall look at what truth is, and then at the conflict of truth versus anti-truth throughout mankind's history. In the coming of Jesus, we recognize that God the Father sent His only-begotten Son into the world to be "the Way, the Truth and the Life" (John 14:6) for all those who would believe in Him. In turn, Jesus has sent the Spirit of Truth from His Heavenly Father to be with us. It is His role as the Advocate to help us resist untruth while at the same time bringing us to the fullness of truth (cf. John 15:26; 16:13). As our Advocate, the Holy Spirit is truly our Counselor, Defender, and Comforter.

CHAPTER 1

TRUTH AND REALITY

*The titles given to the Holy Spirit must surely stir the soul
of anyone who hears them, and make him realize that
they speak of nothing less than the supreme Being. Is he
not called the Spirit of God, the Spirit of truth who pro-
ceeds from the Father, the steadfast Spirit, the guiding
Spirit?*

—St. Basil the Great
The Treatise On the Holy Spirit

IN VIEW OF THE CONFUSION THAT abounds today
concerning truth, it is important that we reflect for a
moment on what we mean when we speak about it. This
is so crucial at the present time in history since every
person—especially each Christian—is caught up in an
immense struggle between truth and the forces opposing
it. And whether he or she consciously knows it or not, each
person must, and eventually will, stand up and take sides in
the conflict.

1

REALITY IS THE FOUNDATION OF TRUTH

If the question is asked, "What is truth?" the way I would like to begin to answer is by saying that truth is related to reality! In other words, if someone or something really exists and I come to know that person or thing as they actually are, then I could say that person or thing is "real." Then my knowledge of that person or thing is "true." For example, when I believe in my mind that St. Peter is one of the twelve Apostles, then my knowledge would be true because St. Peter really is an Apostle. In this case, what I know in my mind corresponds to what exists in reality.

On the other hand, if I have knowledge in my mind of persons or things I think exist but actually are "not real," then my knowledge must be called false or "untrue." For example, if I believe that alien creatures from Mars have landed somewhere on earth, then my knowledge would have to be called "untrue" since such creatures from Mars are not real. In this case, the thought in my mind does not correspond to the reality of the facts. Such an "untruth" would even have to be viewed as a distortion of reality.

GOD ALONE IS THE ULTIMATE REALITY

Now God alone is the ultimate reality. He alone did not receive reality from anyone or anything else. He was never created. He was always real. He always existed. Furthermore, He alone is eternal, because He never had a beginning and He will never have an end! He alone is infinitely perfect, since there are no limits to His divine nature and divine perfections.

This is clearly seen when God revealed His Name to Moses at the burning bush (cf. Exodus 3) at the time He was calling Moses to lead His people out of slavery in Egypt.

> "But," said Moses to God, "when I go to the Israelites and say to them, 'The God of your fathers has sent me to you,' if they ask me, 'What is His Name?' what am I to tell them?" God replied, "I AM WHO AM." Then He added, "This is what you shall tell the Israelites: I AM sent me to you." (Exodus 3:13-14)

This sacred name, "I AM WHO AM" indicates that God can neither change nor cease to exist. He will always be what He has been from all eternity. He is the eternal NOW! He is the same, yesterday, today and forever (cf. Hebrews 13:8). God will always be God!

All That Is Created Receives Its Reality from God

Now, if God alone has reality in Himself, then all His creatures must have received their reality from Him! They had to be created by God, since He alone existed at the beginning of time. Until He created them, they were not yet real, but were mere "possibilities" in the mind of God. All creatures, then, had to be given a reality they did not have before God actually created them.

The vast majority of God's creatures automatically become whatever God created them to be. For example, a lion cub will always become a lion; it cannot decide to become a lamb. If a person plants an apple tree, he should not look for bananas to grow on it. The reality of every animal, vegetable, and mineral creature is already pre-determined by God. They have no choice but to be what God created them to be! They have no option to choose otherwise.

Rational Creatures Must Choose to be Real and True

But God made two of His creatures, angels and men, in such a way that they do have an option to choose to be real or not, to be what God wants them to be or not. Both were given intelligence (to know their options) and free will (to choose as they wish among their options). Since only angels and men among all of God's creatures are capable of love, God has put each of them to the test so that they might choose to love Him above all things by living His commandments. By doing so, they would become fully the reality God wanted them each to be. They would become, as St. Irenaeus once put it, "fully alive."

God Alone Is the Measure of All Truth

Since God alone is Eternal Reality, then He alone is All-Truth in Himself. He is also the measure of truth for all His creatures, since they become real to the extent that they become what He intended them to be. Now only angels and men, as we have just seen, can freely choose to be the reality God intended them to be. Moreover, they will be "in the truth" or "living the truth" to the extent that they love God and keep His commandments. Perhaps a thought from St. Francis of Assisi will help to clarify this idea even more. When people would praise him as a great saint, he would say, "I am what I am in the sight of God, and nothing more!" In other words, God sees and measures the reality of who I am, and that's the "truth"!

We Must Come to Know the Truth

Now, we can be said to be "True" (or authentic human beings) to the extent that we become the reality God wants us to be. We do this by loving and serving the Lord faithfully. But in addition to "being true," we must also come to "know the truth." This is critically important because it is only by knowing the truth about God as well as about ourselves that we can know the purpose for which God has created us and how we might attain the goal—eternal life—to which He is calling each of us. Therefore, we must each seriously seek the truth in order to know it, love it, commit ourselves to it and live by it.

> Man tends by nature toward the truth. He is obliged to honor and bear witness to it: "It is in accordance with their dignity that all men, because they are persons . . . are both impelled by their nature and bound by a moral obligation to seek the truth, especially religious truth. They are also bound to adhere to the truth once they come to know it and direct their whole lives in accordance with the demands of truth." (*Catechism of the Catholic Church*, #2467)

To "seek the truth" and to "live the truth" is what God from the very beginning created us to do. By living the truth that He revealed to us, we would reach the fullness of our human reality, namely, to share God's joy in the Kingdom of Heaven. However, as we shall now see, the truth God intended from the very beginning for all mankind was seriously disturbed, we may even say distorted. As a result, we now find ourselves engaged in an endless struggle between "truth" and "anti-truth." At the same time, however, we are not without hope that truth—the truth that is God Himself and that He has revealed to us—will ultimately emerge victorious!

REFLECTION QUESTIONS

1. Man can be said to be a truly authentic human being only to the extent that he becomes all that God intends him to be. Does your life reflect this reality? Are you "being" everything God intends you to be?

2. What does being "fully alive" mean to you? Can you give a specific example of what that might look like in your life?

3. God sees and measures the reality of who you are—that's the truth. Reflect for a moment on how God sees you. Do you see yourself the way He does?

4. Do you seriously hunger for truth in your life? In what ways are you striving to seek after it?

Holy Spirit, make my heart open to the word of God, make my heart open to goodness, make my heart open to the beauty of God every day.

—POPE FRANCIS

CHAPTER 2

THE CONFLICT BETWEEN
TRUTH & ANTI-TRUTH

Society today is being fragmented by a way of thinking
that is inherently short-sighted because it disregards the
full horizon of truth—the truth about God and about
us. By its nature, relativism fails to see the whole picture.
It ignores the very principles that enable us to live and
flourish in unity, order and harmony.

—Pope Emeritus Benedict XVI
World Youth Day Vigil, July 19, 2008

THE CONFLICT BETWEEN "truth" and its distortion or neglect—let us call it in general "anti-truth" or
falsehood—is not really new. It actually traces back, according to Sacred Scripture, throughout the long centuries of
God's dealings with His people, all the way back to the very
beginning of the human race. Our first parents were pre-
sented with the choice between truth and anti-truth. We
have felt the effects of their choice ever since in what we call
"Original Sin." We are, in a sense, heirs of a conflict which
is rooted in the times and events of the Old Testament but

which continues even now unabated throughout the New Testament era, right up to the present experience of the Catholic Church.

ADAM AND EVE ARE PUT TO THE TEST

What was the choice of our first parents between truth and falsehood or anti-truth? Sacred Scripture presents it in a drama clear and simple. After creating Adam, God put his love for Him to the test by a command of obedience.

> The Lord God took the man and put him in the garden of Eden, to cultivate and care for it. Then the Lord God gave the man this command: "You may freely eat from any of the trees of the garden except the tree of the knowledge of good and evil. From that tree you shall not eat; the moment you eat from it you are surely doomed to die." (Genesis 2:15-17)

When God had created Eve, she, too, felt obliged by the Lord God's command. This command was truth for Adam and Eve. It was the reality God wanted them to live. It was what He knew was better for them. If they "lived the truth" by observing His command, they would be filled with the Lord's joy and remain in His peace. On the other hand, to "reject the truth" by transgressing God's command would bring them sorrow and untold suffering. The stage was set! God's adversary, Lucifer, a fallen angel, victim of his own pride and self-deceit, had led a number of the angels into rebellion against God Himself. He now came to tempt Adam and Eve,[1] to turn them also, if possible, away from God.

THE DEVIL'S TEMPTATION
WAS A DISTORTION OF TRUTH

Satan was the "Deceiver," the "Father of lies." He would tempt Adam and Eve by a distortion of the truth. Since he was now deprived forever of God's joy and peace, he was envious of the joyful and peaceful reality they were enjoying. He wanted to deprive them of their happiness forever. He would use all the cunning and deceit possible on his unsuspecting victims:

> Now the serpent (= Satan) was more cunning than any of the animals that the Lord God had made. The serpent asked the woman, "Did God really tell you not to eat from any of the trees in the garden?" The woman answered the serpent,

---

1   Sacred Scripture states very clearly that Satan and his fallen angels, intent on destroying the Church, are waging a constant spiritual warfare against Her:

> Then war broke out in Heaven. Michael and his angels fought against the dragon. The dragon and his angels fought back but they were defeated and no longer had a place in Heaven. Then the huge dragon—the ancient serpent who is called the Devil or Satan, who deceived the whole world—was hurled down to earth and his minions were cast down with him . . . The dragon went off to wage war . . . on those who keep God's commandments and accept the testimony of Jesus. (Revelations 12:7-9, 17)

> "We may eat of the fruit of the trees in the garden; but God said about the fruit of the tree in the middle of the garden, 'You shall not eat it or even touch it, lest you die.'" (Genesis 3:1-3)

The process of deceit often begins by calling the truth into question.[2] It all seems so harmless to discuss and so curious to consider. One can almost hear the Tempter saying, "Did God really . . . ???" He has now achieved his first goal: the truth has been brought into question! The immediate consequence of this seemingly "harmless questioning" is that the determination to stand by the truth steadfastly has been weakened. The stage is now set for a further assault on the truth. The next step in the dismantling of truth is to convince people that no harm will come from doing away with the truth:

> But the serpent said to the woman: "You will not die! God knows well that the moment you eat of it your eyes will be opened, and you will be like gods who know what is good and what is evil." (Genesis 3:4-5)

Once the Deceiver convinces our first parents that no harm will come to them for neglecting the "truth" of God's command, he adds to his deception by false promises of

---

2   Someone once described how the subtlety of a lie works:

First, it makes us question (the truth).
Then we tolerate it.
Then we embrace it!

spectacular benefits that will actually happen to them: "You will be like gods." Since he himself had sinned by pride, he knows how strong the attraction to pride and vanity can be! This deception subtly lies at the basis of every temptation: to become like gods! At creation, God made man in His own image and likeness (cf. Genesis 1:26), but throughout human history, man has been constantly tempted to remake God into his own image and likeness, substituting either himself as "god" or at least an image of a "god" he can live with comfortably and who makes no unwanted demands upon him. Man succumbs to this temptation every time he moves away from God's truth. Once this stage is reached in the temptation, the deceit becomes complete!

> The woman saw that the tree was good for food, a delight to the eyes, and desirable for gaining wisdom. (Genesis 3:6)

There is an old saying: "Forbidden fruit always looks more appealing." Once the resistance of the intellect to falsehood has broken down, the senses tune in and seek their own satisfaction. What is forbidden looks so appealing in every way—for sensual pleasure ("good for food"), for aesthetical beauty ("a delight to the eyes"), and for intellectual benefit ("desirable for gaining wisdom"). The attraction to evil has now gone from the mind into the heart. The attraction to falsehood and deception has now become very "personal": "This will satisfy ME!" There now remains only the external carrying out of evil, rejecting truth and embracing a lie:

So she took some of its fruit and ate it; and she
also gave some to her husband, who was with her,
and he ate it. Then the eyes of both of them were
opened, and they realized that they were naked;
so they sewed fig leaves together and made loin-
cloths for themselves. (Genesis 3:6-7)

THE EVIL CONSEQUENCES OF
FALSEHOOD AND SIN

The effects of their sin were not long in coming for Adam
and Eve! Their eyes were immediately opened, and they realized their nakedness! The tranquil love, joy, peace, and security they enjoyed with God, with each other and with nature
around them was lost! Now they hid from God in their guilt
and from each other in their shame (cf. Genesis 3:8-13).
Now they would struggle with nature, Adam tilling the fields
in the sweat of his brow and Eve giving birth in the great
pangs of childbirth (cf. Genesis 3:16-19). Other sorrows
would later follow: envy, hatred, and murder as seen in the
incident of Cain killing his brother Abel (cf. Genesis 4:1-16).
Still later, stirred by a rebellious pride, people became further
alienated from God and from one another, as is seen in the
story of the Tower of Babel (cf. Genesis 11:1-9).

What followed from these experiences is literally all of
human history. It is the history of the human race down
through the centuries, now caught in an unending struggle
between the forces of good and evil, of light and darkness, of
life and death itself. It is a human history wounded by "Original Sin." It is a human history where the deceit of the Evil

One has brought falsehood in all its forms—ignorance, lies, distortion, and perversion to name a few—to contaminate the pure truth in which God had created our first parents and in which He intended all their children, including ourselves, to live. Like a person who contracts malaria, which is never fully removed from the body but at best is held in check by proper diet, medication, and a strong immune system, so falsehood has entered into the human situation, in some cases tainting, while in many other cases contaminating, the very purity itself of the truth God revealed to His People. Only God, Who is Truth and the Source of all Truth for us, can restore the pristine purity of truth in human history. The *Catechism of the Catholic Church* states clearly:

> God is Truth itself, whose words cannot deceive. This is why one can abandon oneself in full trust to the truth and faithfulness of His word in all things. The beginning of sin and of man's fall was due to a lie of the tempter who induced doubt of God's word, kindness and faithfulness. (#215)

THE "ANTI-TRUTH"

Pope St. John Paul II, in his encyclical letter on the Holy Spirit, *Dominum et vivificantem,* gives us an even deeper insight into how Original Sin has turned man to a certain degree away from God, his Creator. He also shows how it has sown into man's heart a certain sense of "suspicion" against God's goodness along with a certain attraction to that vain desire "to be like God," which the Devil, the "father of lies," used to lead our first parents into sin. The Holy Father sees all of this as the "anti-truth":

> According to the witness of the beginning, God in creation has revealed Himself as omnipotence, which is love. At the same time He has revealed to Man that, as the "image and likeness" of his Creator, he is called to participate in truth and love. This participation means a life in union with God, Who is "eternal life." But man, under the influence of the "father of lies," has separated himself from this participation. To what degree? Certainly not to the degree of the sin of a pure spirit, to the degree of the sin of Satan. The human spirit is incapable of reaching such a degree . . .
>
> Man's disobedience, nevertheless, always means a turning away from God, and in a certain sense the closing up of human freedom (with regard to God). It also means a certain opening of this freedom—of the human mind and will—to the one who is the "father of lies." This act of conscious choice is not only "disobedience," but it also involves a certain consent to the motivation which was contained in the first temptation to sin and which is unceasingly renewed during the whole history of man on earth: "For God knows that when you eat of (the tree) your eyes will be opened, and you will be like God, knowing good and evil."

Here we find ourselves at the very center of what could be called the "anti-Word," that is to say, the "anti-truth." For the truth about man becomes falsified: who man is and what are the impassable limits of his being and freedom. This "anti-truth" (about man) is possible because at the same time there is a complete falsification of the truth about Who God is. God the Creator is placed in a state of suspicion, indeed of accusation, in the mind of the creature. For the first time in human history there appears the perverse "genius of suspicion" (= the Devil). He seeks to "falsify" Good itself, the absolute Good (= God), which precisely in the work of creation has manifested itself as the Good which gives itself in an inexpressible way: . . . as creative love. (*Dominum et vivificantem*, par. #37, pp. 64-66)

A Ray of Hope Dawns for Mankind

Was there any hope left for man and woman to return from this place of the "anti-Truth" to which sin had reduced them, to that place of the "Truth" where they would once again correctly know who they really were as creatures and Who God really was as Creator? For their part, man and woman could not solve this tragic situation. But God could, and He did! No sooner had Adam and Eve sinned than God promises to send a "Savior." The Original Sin thus becomes, as St. Augustine described it, a *felix culpa*, a happy fault. Why? Because it merits for us so great a blessing that the Son of God Himself would become man to save us from our sins. Ironically, God foretells the coming of this "Savior" in words He addresses to the very tempter who has just succeeded in deceiving our first parents to sin:

> I will put enmity between you and the Woman, and between your offspring and hers; He will strike at your head, while you strike at His heel. (Genesis 3:15)

The Church sees this promise as a prophetic passage. The "Woman" is the Blessed Virgin Mary, who will become a "New Eve" in God's plan of salvation. Her "offspring" is Jesus. He is God's Son and now Mary's Son as well. Jesus, as the "New Adam" (cf. 1 Corinthians 15:45), will destroy the power of Satan, man's deceiver, along with that of his followers, by His own saving Death and Resurrection. This "salvation" will begin the destruction of falsehood and the restoration of Truth for all men and women.

The Hope of the Old Testament Covenant

God faithfully prepared for the sending of His Divine Son into the world. His solicitude for our well-being and salvation has continued unabated over the centuries. The Church expresses this in her Liturgy:

> Even when (man) disobeyed You and lost Your friendship, You did not abandon him to the power of death. . . . Again and again You offered a covenant to man. (*Roman Missal*, Eucharistic Prayer IV, 118)

God made one covenant[3] with Abraham (cf. Genesis 15) who, because of his great faith, was to be the "father of all who believe" (cf. Romans 5:16). Through Abraham, God was to make the Jewish people His "chosen people," from whom the promised Savior of the world would come. God made another covenant with Moses at Mt. Sinai (cf. Exodus 19-24). This covenant formed Israel into a close knit covenant people. Under Moses' leadership, God directed His People from slavery in Egypt to freedom in the Promised

---

3   A covenant was a solemn pact or agreement made between two parties who pledged certain promises to one another. These covenants could be made between individuals, families, clans, or nations. They were very common in the Near East in biblical times. They were necessary to regulate social behavior in regard to mutual respect for property, for maintaining peace, and the like, especially because there were no international laws at the time regulating these matters.

In covenants, the two consenting parties usually made certain pledges to one another, promising to fulfill certain obligations (e.g., pay a tribute) or refrain from certain forms of activity (for example, war or plunder). These covenants would be sealed with oaths (for example, asking the "gods" of that nation to bless or punish the contracting parties if they fulfilled or neglected the pledges made in the covenant) and often with a ceremony called "the cutting of a covenant," in which an animal was sacrificed and its blood was sprinkled on the covenanting parties. This blood "sealed" the covenant pact.

In the Old Testament, God entered into a covenant with Israel. He promised to be their God Who cared for them with special solicitude. They, in turn, were to be His Chosen People, who obligated themselves to worship Him alone and to keep His commandments. In the New Testament, Jesus established the new and eternal covenant between God and His Church, which He sealed with His own Precious Blood shed for us by His redemptive suffering and death on the Cross.

Land. To Israel, God revealed the Truth of His Law as part of the Covenant. A third covenant (2 Samuel 7:5-16) God made with His servant, David, called as a young boy from caring for his father's flock to shepherd God's People, Israel. Despite the struggles caused by years of war and even lapses into personal sin, David deeply loved God and served Him with a genuinely "humble and contrite heart" (Psalm 51:1-9). God rewarded King David's love with the promise that one of his royal descendants would be a King forever, a reference to Jesus' eternal Kingship.

During all of these long centuries from Abraham through Moses and David down to Jesus,[4] God gradually revealed Himself, His "truth" and plan of salvation to His People. Especially through His prophets, God taught the message of truth and the way of salvation to the degree the Old Testament Chosen People were capable of grasping that message of Truth. The Spirit of Truth was inspiring the message of these holy prophets. As we say in the Nicene Creed, "we believe in the Holy Spirit . . . He has spoken through the prophets."

Jesus Comes in the Fullness of Time

Finally, in that mysterious "fullness of time," God fulfilled the promises of His covenants and the messages of His prophets by sending His own Divine Son into the world. In the person and mission of Jesus, God the Father would speak His definitive Word of Truth:

---

4   Historians estimate this period of time to be anywhere between 1400-2000 years.

> In times past, God spoke in fragmentary and var-
> ied ways to our fathers through the prophets; in
> this, the final age, He has spoken to us through
> His Son . . . (Hebrews 1:1-2)

JESUS IS THE "TRUTH"

Now the fullness of God's Truth is found in Jesus. First of all, He Who is true God and true man proclaimed Himself to be the "Truth": "I Am the Way, and the Truth, and the Life!" (John 14:6). St. Paul tells us that Jesus is the very fullness of truth, of reality, for He is the very "image of the invisible God" (Colossians 1:15) and in Him dwells the fullness of Divinity (cf. Colossians 2:9).

> In Jesus Christ, the whole of God's truth has been
> made manifest. "Full of grace and truth." He came
> as the "Light of the world," He is the Truth (John
> 1:14; 8:12; cf. 14:6). "Whoever believes in Me may
> not remain in darkness" (John 12:46). The disciple
> of Jesus continues in His word so as to know "the
> truth [that] will make you free" and that sanctifies
> (John 8:32; cf. 17:17). (*Catechism of the Catholic
> Church*, #2466. p. 591)

Belief in Jesus as the truth is absolutely essential because it leads us to eternal life:

> When we pray for you we always give thanks to
> God, the Father of our Lord Jesus Christ, because
> we have heard of your faith in Christ Jesus and of

your love for all the saints—moved as you are by
the hope stored up for you in Heaven. You first
heard of this hope through the message of truth,
the Gospel, which has come to you, has borne
fruit, and has continued to grow in your midst, as
it has everywhere in the world. (Colossians 1:3-6)

Jesus is the Teacher of Truth

Jesus is not only the fullness of the Father's truth in the world,
but He is also the Teacher of all truth. He tells us all that we
need to know to cooperate with His grace in working out our
salvation and sanctification. With St. Peter, we must exclaim:

Lord, to whom would we go? You have the words
of eternal life. We have come to believe and are
convinced that You are the Holy One of God.
(John 6:68)

Jesus Himself tells us that those who hear His words and
live by the truths He teaches us are like wise men who build
their houses on a solid rock foundation. When the storms of
life come and afflict that person, his dwelling built on solid
rock will endure; the truths he has heard from Jesus will be
his life's support. In contrast, those who hear His voice but
do not heed His word or live by His truths, Jesus compares
to foolish men who build their houses on sand. When the
storms of life hit these houses, they collapse under the pres-
sures of life (cf. Matthew 7:24-27). The solid and enduring
foundation of truth was missing!

"I WILL SEND YOU THE SPIRIT OF TRUTH . . ."

Jesus has now returned to His Heavenly Kingdom, to reign in glory at the right hand of His Eternal Father. So, then, how can we now come to know Jesus as the "Truth" Who gives meaning and reality to our lives? Furthermore, how can we come to know the many specific truths He taught us to direct us in working out our salvation and sanctification?

The answer is twofold. First, it is through the teachings of the Roman Catholic Church, which Jesus founded upon the rock of St. Peter and his inspired profession of faith: "You are the Christ, the Son of the Living God" (Matthew 16:16). This special teaching authority is the result of the enlightenment and guidance of the Holy Spirit, Who has been poured forth upon the Church. Jesus gave the Spirit of Truth in a special way to the leaders of His Church, to St. Peter and the Apostles as well as to their successors today, the pope and the bishops in union with him. They received the Holy Spirit in a special way by their episcopal consecration so that they might fulfill the threefold responsibility they have by their hierarchical offices, namely: to teach, to sanctify, and to govern all the faithful of Christ.

Second, the Holy Spirit has also been given to all the faithful of the Church. He comes first by our Baptism through which we receive new life in Christ. It is the Spirit's presence and work in us that enables us to live our Christian lives faithfully and grow in the holiness to which we have been called as adopted children of God (cf. Romans 8:14-17). He then comes again through our Confirmation, which gives us a certain maturity in professing and defending our

Catholic Faith by giving witness to Christ through our words as well as our deeds. We must join the struggle in the world today between "truth" and "anti-truth," between the Catholic Church and those who oppose Her, Her truth and Her mission. In this struggle the Lord Jesus has not left us to our own resources. He has given us the Holy Spirit, Whom He also called the Spirit of Truth, to continue to guide His Church until He returns at the end of time.

Let us now look more closely at how the Spirit of Truth fulfills His great mission in our lives by becoming our Advocate!

REFLECTION QUESTIONS

1. Throughout human history, man has constantly given in to the temptation to remake God into his own image and likeness. Are there any areas in your life where this is true? Can you cite some examples?

2. Have you been building your "house" on a solid rock foundation, so that, despite the storms of life, your "house" endures? Are the truths that you have heard from Jesus, through the Church, your life's support?

3. Are there any truths of the Church that you struggle with, or even reject? What are they? Do you pray to the Spirit of Truth to help you see things more clearly?

*Most Holy Spirit! Receive the
consecration that I make of my entire
being. From this moment on, come into
every area of my life and into each of my
actions. You are my Light, my Guide, my
Strength and the sole desire of my heart.
I abandon myself without reservation to
your divine action, and I desire to be ever
docile to Your inspirations.*

*Oh Holy Spirit! Transform me with
and through Mary, into another Christ
Jesus, for the glory of the Father and the
salvation of the world. AMEN.*

—SERVANT OF GOD FELIX DE JESÚS ROUGIER, M.SP.S.

CHAPTER 3

THE SPIRIT OF TRUTH
IS THE ADVOCATE

*Thus the Paraclete, the Spirit of truth, is man's true
Counselor. Thus He is the true Defender and Advocate.
He is the guarantor of the Gospel in history. Under His
influence, the good news is always the same and always
near, and in an ever new way He illumines man's path
in the perspective of heaven with "words of eternal life"
(John 6:68).*

—Pope St. John Paul II
General Audience, May 17, 1989

SEVERAL TIMES DURING THE Last Supper account in
the Gospel of St. John, Our Lord refers to the Holy Spirit
as the Paraclete. This is a very important title for the Holy
Spirit, so let us look closely at it to understand clearly what
this title means. The word "paraclete" comes from ancient
Greek usage. The Greek word literally meant "someone
called to the side (of another)." Jesus Himself had been a "paraclete" to His disciples since He had been at their side during
the three years of His public ministry. Now that He was about

to return to His Heavenly Father, He did not want to leave them all alone: "I will not leave you orphaned" (John 14:18). He wanted someone else to be with His disciples who would take His place at their side. So He promises them that His Heavenly Father will give "another Paraclete," the Holy Spirit:

> I will ask the Father and He will give you another Paraclete to be with you always. (John 14:16)

In reference to the Holy Spirit, the title "the Paraclete" has been expressed in English in a number of ways.[1] For example, it is often rendered as "the Comforter" or "the Consoler" because of the comfort and consolation He brings us. But the title that comes closest to the biblical meaning is "the Advocate." "Advocate" is from the Latin *ad,* which means "to" or "towards," and *vocatus,* which means "one called." So "advocate" literally translates the word "paraclete" in the sense of "someone called to (the side of) another." There is even another striking similarity between the words "paraclete"

---

1   Other expressions used to translate the word "paraclete" include:

(1) The Counselor, because of the wise counsel or advice He gives us to make the best choices in our Christian lives:

(2) The Guide, because He directs all the ministries and other activities of the Church as a whole, as well as in our personal lives:

(3) The Helper, since He assists us in all our undertakings, especially when our own resources seem so inadequate and we are most in need—St. Paul says He "helps us in our weakness" (Romans 8:26):

(4) The Teacher, because He instructs us in all the ways and truths of our Christian lives:

(5) The Intercessor, because as St. Paul writes, He "makes intersession for us with groanings that cannot be expressed in speech," and He "intercedes for the saints as God Himself wills." (Romans 8:26-27)

and "advocate." In popular speech among the ancient Greeks the word "paraclete" meant a "lawyer." In ancient Latin usage, "advocate" also referred to a "lawyer." Thus, these two words are also similar since they both originally referred to a "lawyer."

This gives us a key to understanding more fully the role of the Spirit of Truth in our lives. Now, what does a lawyer do for his clients? Basically, there are two roles a lawyer can play, namely, that of a defense lawyer, and that of a prosecuting attorney. The works of the Holy Spirit as the Advocate resemble both roles. Let us now reflect on how each applies to the working of the Holy Spirit.

THE ADVOCATE DEFENDS
US FROM ANTI-TRUTH

A good lawyer, first of all, defends his clients from accusations made against them. As a defense attorney, he points out any inaccuracies or, even more so, deliberate distortions in the charges being made against his clients. In this way, his clients are protected from such false accusations. In a similar way, the Advocate defends us when accusations are made against us as followers of Jesus. These accusations might include attacks on the teachings of the Church in order to distort them, thereby trying to misrepresent them as either wrong, or contradictory, or outdated, or simply unrealistic. The Holy Spirit, as our Advocate, defends us when Church teachings are attacked by assisting us to recognize or discern where such distortions are false and then to resist and counter these false accusations by the light of His truth.

The Advocate Helps Us
to Promote the Truth

Another thing a good lawyer does is to assist his clients when
there is a need to initiate a legal case or carry out some legal
transaction. In other words, not only does a lawyer fulfill a
"defensive" role in protecting his clients, but he also fulfills
an "offensive" role when these same clients begin some legal
procedure. In this sense, we speak of a prosecuting attorney.
He acts as the clients' spokesman to promote their cause. In
a similar way, the Holy Spirit assists us in spreading the message of Jesus throughout the world. He is our "Spokesman"
in promoting the work of evangelization. He furthermore
confirms the authentic teaching of the Church by the inner
light of truth which He gives to those who "hear the word in
a spirit of openness, retain it, and bear fruit through perse-
verance" (Luke 8:15). Oftentimes, He confirms the truth of
the Church's message by working "signs and wonders" (cf.
Acts 2:43; 5:12) at the hands of those who are witnessing to
Christ. Sometimes these "signs and wonders" may be miraculous, as often happened in the lives of the saints. Most of
the times, however, it might have been in the form of great
deeds of charity,[2] or holiness of life,[3] or works of mercy which
gave a powerful witness to others,[4] or simply a sense of peace

---

2 This was the case with St. Teresa of Calcutta.
3 St. Thérèse of Lisieux would exemplify holiness of life.
4 When St. Maximilian Mary Kolbe gave his life for a condemned man
   in the Nazi concentration camp at Auschwitz, he gave a witness of
   Christian love and mercy to the Nazi officer, as well as all the prison-
   ers in the camp.

and joy in the life of the person witnessing to Jesus in his or her life.[5]

No one can believe in Jesus and in the truths He taught in His lifetime and which He continues to teach through His Church without the grace of faith. To accept a belief as true, a person must be given the inner enlightenment to recognize that what is being taught is correct, that it corresponds to what is real. Initial faith does not require that we understand a certain teaching completely; that comes gradually with further knowledge and understanding and experience. But faith does require that what is proposed as truth is not contradictory. To paraphrase a sign in the window of a Catholic bookstore in London, England: "We are not able to give you faith, but we can certainly correct any misunderstandings you may have."

The Holy Spirit must give the inner realization or enlightenment that the belief being preached comes from God and is therefore worthy of acceptance. St. Paul speaks of this realization or awareness, this inner "witness" of the Holy Spirit, when he writes:

> The Spirit Himself bears witness with our spirit
> that we are God's children. (Romans 8:16)

The role of the Spirit of Truth extends even further than His inner witness in our hearts. He would also give witness to Jesus along with the visible witness of the Apostles:

> When the Advocate comes, whom I will send to
> you from the Father—the Spirit of truth Who

---

5 Hopefully, many of us can give this kind of witness in our daily lives.

comes forth from the Father—He will bear witness on My behalf. You must bear witness as well, because you have been with Me from the beginning. (John 15:26-27)

The Advocate, the Spirit of Truth, helps us in our cause, which is to promote the truth of Christ. He assists us to spread the truth Christ has taught us to every person. He tells us what to say by first convicting us personally with the truth, and then by inspiring us and prompting us to want to share that same truth with others.

The Experience of St. Paul

St. Paul gives us a clear teaching on how the Holy Spirit helps us to come to know the truth personally. He presents this in his First Letter to the Corinthians. It will be helpful if we begin by reviewing briefly a little of the background to the situation that caused St. Paul to write to the Corinthians. The Apostle of the Gentiles had come to Corinth and established the Church there after preaching at Athens. His preaching experience in Athens ended disastrously. He spoke in the famous Areopagus,[6] before a crowd of intellectuals. He even quoted from Greek philosophers to accommodate more easily his message to his cultured Greek audience. However, when he began to preach about the bodily resurrection of Jesus from the dead and the resurrection of our own bodies

---

6   The Areopagus was the governing council of Athens. It was so named from the fact that the council held its meetings on a hill in Athens named for Ares, or Mars. It was here that St. Paul delivered his famous address to the Athenians (cf. Acts 17:22).

when Jesus comes again, they laughed at him. There is no doubt that St. Paul was a deeply religious person, but I also believe he was very sensitive as well. This ridicule must have hurt him deeply. It affected him so much that it filled him with a certain fear and trepidation as he approached Corinth to preach there. If they had ridiculed him in Athens with its reputation for openness to "new ideas" (cf. Acts 17:16-34, esp. 19-21), what could he, humanly speaking, hope to achieve in Corinth with its reputation for being a "sin city"? After all, Corinth, even by pagan standards, was a wide open city, with vice and immorality abounding. Wasn't it the center of the immoral cult of Aphrodite, the so-called goddess of love? Despite his anxiety, when St. Paul did preach at Corinth, he ironically had amazing success. His approach was different from that at Athens. He did not go there and preach with any "worldly argument" or philosophical eloquence, nor did he try to quote any pagan authors. He simply preached the core of the Christian message: Jesus crucified. In this alone, he said, could be found the wisdom and the power of God.

Now, once the Church was established by St. Paul at Corinth, its growth was fostered by a powerful evangelist named Apollos, a convert from Judaism. As time passed, however, the effects of fallen and weak human nature made themselves felt in the young Church community at Corinth. The disciples began to be divided in their loyalties, forming "cliques" around the great leaders of the Church there. Some claimed they were for Paul, others for Apollos, still others for Peter (called Cephas), and some even went so far as to state they were for Christ! Now, love brings together, it does

31

not divide.[7] These divisions convinced St. Paul that many of the Corinthians were spiritually still very immature. So, he calls them still "infants in Christ," not mature adults. He then introduces the idea that there is a true wisdom, but only for those who mature in their life in Christ:

> There is, to be sure, a certain wisdom which we express among the spiritually mature. It is not a wisdom of this age, however, nor of the rulers of this age who are men headed for destruction. Instead what we preach is God's wisdom; a mysterious, a hidden wisdom . . . Of this wisdom it is written: "Eye has not seen; ear has not heard, nor has it so much as dawned on man what God has prepared for those who love Him." Yet God has revealed this wisdom to us through the Spirit. (1 Corinthians 2:6-7; 9-10)

St. Paul contrasts the "wisdom of the world" with the "wisdom of the Spirit." The wisdom of this world cannot lead to eternal life. but only to eternal death. It has its focus on this world alone. Furthermore, it cannot grasp the truth of Jesus' message which requires that one look beyond this earthly life. St. Paul was to experience this limitation of worldly wisdom very often in his preaching mission. He had found that the Jewish people were expecting a powerful earthly Messiah who would overthrow the Romans and reestablish the splendor of the kingdom of Israel as it was under Kings David

---

7   St. Paul would give his beautiful description of "love" in chapter 13 of this letter.

and Solomon. Instead, he preached to the Jews that their own leaders in the Sanhedrin had condemned Jesus, the Messiah, and handed Him over to the Romans to be put to death. As a result, when he preached Christ crucified to the Jews, they found this message a "stumbling block."

In contrast, he found that the Greeks were looking for worldly "wisdom." So, when he preached to them the message of "Christ crucified," stressing that God died at the hands of His own creatures, the Greeks found such a message "complete foolishness" and "utter absurdity." But he also found that whenever individuals, whether they were Jews or Greeks, were open to his message about "Christ crucified," they understood Jesus to be truly "the power of God and the wisdom of God" (1 Corinthians 1:24).

The Spirit of Truth Assists Us to Grow in the Truth

St. Paul drew from this experience his teaching on how the Holy Spirit reveals this wisdom and power of God to us. He makes a contrast. On the one hand, there is the "spiritual man" who is open to the message of "Jesus crucified" and accepts the light of the Spirit to help him grasp the true "wisdom of God." The "spiritual man," because he possesses this special light of the Spirit's wisdom, can discern the truth of all things. Furthermore, he can judge correctly the values as well as the conduct (= lifestyle) that lead to life as opposed to those which lead to death.

On the other hand, there is the "natural man" who, lacking the light and wisdom of the Holy Spirit, can only judge by the limited and often distorted wisdom of this world alone. Therefore, this "natural man" cannot understand what the "spiritual man" believes or why he does so. He cannot even understand that his own distorted moral values are leading him to separation from "the true and living God" into the service of idols and ultimately, subjection to "dead gods" of his own choice and making. St. Paul sums up:

> The Spirit is able to scrutinize everything, even the depths of God's intentions. Who can know what someone else intends? Surely only that person's own spirit knows! So, too, no one knows what God intends except the Spirit of God. But the Spirit we have received is not the spirit of this world but the Spirit that comes from God and enables us to know what it is that God has freely bestowed upon us. And we proclaim this, not in words of human wisdom but in words taught by the Spirit, words which explain spiritual matters to those who have the Spirit. The unspiritual man is unable to accept what comes from the Spirit of God, since for him it is foolishness. He cannot understand such matters because they must be evaluated in a spiritual way. The spiritual man, on the other hand, is able to evaluate all such matters and is subject to no one else's judgment. For, "Who knows the mind of God; who can advise Him?" But we have the mind of Christ. (1 Corinthians 2:10-16)

It is because we have been given the Holy Spirit that we can come to the fullness of that wisdom that guides us in living as true children of God in this world, and in coming to the fullness of life God has prepared for us in the Kingdom of Heaven. In our later chapters we will first look in greater detail at the role of the Holy Spirit, the Advocate, as similar to that of a "defense lawyer" assisting us to resist the dangers that threaten to compromise or distort or even destroy the truth that God has revealed to us and that the Catholic Church teaches us. He does this, as we shall see, by helping us to counter the attacks on truth stemming from ignorance, error, and falsehood. Then, we will look at the many roles the Holy Spirit, like a "prosecuting attorney," exercises in fostering the truth. These include helping us to (1) discern the truth, (2) live the truth, (3) proclaim the truth faithfully, and (4) defend the truth. In the following chapters we will focus on each of these roles. However, before we do so, let us look at one other area that has special relation to the work of the Spirit of Truth, and that is the sacrament of Confirmation.

Reflection Questions

1. Are you more often a "spiritual man" or a "natural man"?

2. Do you try to discern the truth in all things?

3. The wisdom of the world, unlike the wisdom of the Spirit, cannot grasp the truth of Jesus' message because it requires that one look beyond this earthly life. Do you often strive to live with the Spirit of wisdom by looking at the circumstances of your life with a supernatural

perspective? Can you cite some practical examples of how you strive to see things with a supernatural outlook?

O God, send forth your Holy Spirit into my heart that I may perceive, into my mind that I may remember, and into my soul that I may meditate. Inspire me to speak with piety, holiness, tenderness, and mercy. Teach, guide, and direct my thoughts and senses from beginning to end. May your grace ever help and correct me, and may I be strengthened now with wisdom from on high, for the sake of your infinite mercy. Amen.

—ST. ANTHONY OF PADUA

CHAPTER 4

THE SPIRIT OF TRUTH AND THE SACRAMENT OF CONFIRMATION

Proclaim the truth and do not be silent through fear.

—St. Catherine of Siena

THE ROLE OF THE ADVOCATE has a special connection with the sacrament of Confirmation. A great deal can be said about this sacrament. Our focus, therefore, will be first a brief look at the rite of Confirmation and its history, and then at how the special work of the Spirit of Truth relates to this sacrament.

CONFIRMATION: PART OF CHRISTIANIZATION

Confirmation, along with Baptism and Holy Eucharist, forms a continuing process of full initiation into the Catholic Church. Baptism, the first act of initiation, confers a new life in Christ "by water and the Spirit" (John 3:5) to those who receive it. Confirmation perfects and completes Baptism by a second conferring of the Holy Spirit in order to strengthen

37

those who receive it to give fearless witness to their Catholic Faith by mature Christian lives. Finally, the Holy Eucharist completes our Christian initiation by providing the very Body and Blood of Jesus Christ as our Food of eternal life, and as the chief means for our ongoing growth and maturity in the Catholic Faith. In summary, we have the origin (= Baptism), the development (= Confirmation) and the nourishing (= Holy Eucharist) of our new spiritual life in Christ.

> Baptism, the Eucharist, and the sacrament of Confirmation together constitute the "sacraments of Christian initiation," whose unity must be safeguarded. It must be explained to the faithful that the reception of the sacrament of Confirmation is necessary for the completion of baptismal grace (cf. *Roman Ritual*, Rite of Confirmation (OC). Introduction 1). For "by the sacrament of Confirmation [the baptized] are more perfectly bound to the Church and are enriched with a special strength of the Holy Spirit. Hence they are, as true witnesses of Christ, more strictly obliged to spread and defend the Faith by word and deed" (cf. *Lumen Gentium* 11; and also OC, Introduction 2). (*Catechism of the Catholic Church*, #1285, pp. 325-326)

SCRIPTURAL EVIDENCE FOR CONFIRMATION

One of the questions theologians studying this sacrament always ask is: "Does Scripture speak of a second gift or

THE SPIRIT OF TRUTH

conferring of the Holy Spirit after Baptism?" Obviously, this question is extremely important. First of all, since the three sacraments of Christian initiation were originally all conferred in the same ceremony, there was question of where Baptism ended and Confirmation began. Secondly, it is extremely important to show from Scripture that the earliest Christians were already receiving this sacrament.

In response to the question at issue, we can state that there is clear evidence for Confirmation in the Acts of the Apostles, which describes life in the very early Church. It was conferred through the gesture referred to as "the laying on of hands" on the head of the person being confirmed. One such example is found in Acts 8:4-17. This account describes how the Apostles Peter and John went to Samaria to impose hands on persons who were recently baptized by Philip, the deacon. By the Apostles imposing their hands, these Samaritans received the Holy Spirit. Another example is found in Acts 19:1-7. Here, St. Paul the Apostle lays hands on twelve Ephesians (former disciples of St. John the Baptist) after they had received the Christian sacrament of Baptism. By this imposition of hands, the Holy Spirit came down upon all of them.

> . . . the Apostles, in fulfillment of Christ's will, imparted to the newly baptized by the laying on of hands the gift of the Spirit that completes the grace of Baptism . . . The imposition of hands is rightly recognized by the Catholic tradition as the origin of the sacrament of Confirmation, which in a certain way perpetuates the grace of

Pentecost in the Church. (Paul VI, *Divinae con-sortium naturae*, 659; cf. Acts 8:15-17; 19:5-6; and Hebrews 6:2, quoted in *Catechism of the Catholic Church*, #1288, p. 326)

ANOINTING WITH OIL WAS ADDED TO THE RITE OF CONFIRMATION

In the early Christian centuries, an anointing with "chrism" (perfumed or aromatic oil) was added to the gesture of the laying on of hands in the sacrament of Confirmation. This anointing helped to signify more clearly the conferring of the Holy Sprit. This anointing emphasized the idea of a "Christian" as a follower of Jesus Who was "the Anointed One," in Hebrew "the Messiah," and in Greek "the Christ." Jesus Himself was "anointed" for His messianic mission when the Holy Spirit came down and rested upon Him at His baptism in the Jordan River.

In addition, anointing with oil has always had, both in the Bible and in ancient usage, a great symbolism. This was especially so for qualities of strength (soldiers before hand-to-hand combat and athletes before competition limbered up with oil), of health (oil was used to soothe and heal wounds), of beauty (oil was used after bathing as a cosmetic, with a fragrance that gave off a pleasing aroma) and of joy (since oil was a sign of abundance).

All of these natural symbolisms of anointing with oil helped to bring out a fuller understanding of the effects of what the anointing by the Holy Spirit in the sacrament of Confirmation does for those who receive it. Confirmation gives us strength to defend our Catholic Faith when it is attacked, as well as the courage to spread it out of love for Jesus, Our Lord, to make Him known and loved by others. Anointing with the Holy Spirit helps to heal the wounds of sin and the bruises of our spiritual warfare by giving us the soothing comfort of His fruits of love and peace. St. Paul reminds us that since we now share through our anointing by the Holy Spirit more completely in the mission of Jesus, our lives must give off "the aroma of Christ" (cf. 2 Corinthians 2:15). Finally, our joy is abundant because we share in the fullness of the Holy Spirit Who is often referred to by the biblical title, the "Oil of Gladness." All of these blessings are so significant that the rite of anointing with chrism has actually determined the name of the sacrament.

> This rite of anointing has continued ever since (the early Christian centuries), in both East and West. For this reason the Eastern Churches call this sacrament Chrismation, anointing with chrism, or myron which means "chrism." In the West, confirmation suggests the ratification of Baptism . . . and the strengthening of baptismal grace—both fruits of the Holy Spirit. (*Catechism of the Catholic Church*, #1289, p. 327)

CONFIRMATION CONFERS A "SEALING" WITH THE HOLY SPIRIT

The anointing with chrism in Confirmation brings out one other very important aspect of the sacrament through which the Spirit of Truth works more completely in our lives. It is the idea that the person who is confirmed receives the "seal" or "mark" of the Holy Spirit. A "seal" represented a person, or his authority, or his ownership of something. For example, the seal of the pope or the president indicates that the documents so sealed actually are the pope's or the president's own. Now in ancient times, soldiers were "marked" or "sealed" (= branded) with their king's seal, as slaves were with their master's seal. So, when a person receives Confirmation, he is "sealed" with the sign of the Holy Spirit as belonging totally to Christ and as being enrolled in His service forever.

> God . . . has placed His seal on us and given our hearts His Spirit as a guarantee. (2 Corinthians 1:22)

This "sealing" (in Latin, *signaculum*) with the Holy Spirit was so significant that it was used as another ancient name for the sacrament itself in the West. It is still today an essential part of the rite of Confirmation in the West. The celebrant of the sacrament (either a bishop or an authorized priest) who confirms, while laying his hand on the head of the person being confirmed, anoints the person's forehead with his thumb which he has dipped into the chrism (sacred aromatic oil), tracing the form of the Sign of the Cross. While he does this, the celebrant says, "(Confirmation Name), receive the seal of the Holy Spirit, the Gift of God."

THE "LAYING ON OF HANDS" IN CONFIRMATION TODAY

Prior to this anointing with the sacred chrism, the bishop (or authorized priest) extends his hands over the whole group to be confirmed and prays that they will receive the Gift of the Holy Spirit. This ceremony recalls and preserves in the sacrament of Confirmation the ancient biblical ceremony of the "laying on of the hands." As the celebrant of Confirmation extends his hands over the group to be confirmed, he prays the following beautiful prayer, asking Our Heavenly Father to send the Holy Spirit and His gifts upon all of them:

> All-powerful God, Father of Our Lord Jesus Christ,
> by water and the Holy Spirit
> You freed Your sons and daughters from sin
> and gave them new life.
> Send Your Holy Spirit upon them
> to be their Helper and Guide
> Give them the Spirit of wisdom and
> understanding,
> the Spirit of right judgment (counsel) and
> courage,
> the Spirit of knowledge and reverence (piety).
> Fill them with the Spirit of wonder and awe (fear
> of the Lord)
> in Your presence.
> We ask this through Christ Our Lord.

> (OC 25; quoted in *Catechism of the Catholic Church*, #1299. p. 329)

SIGNIFICANT HISTORICAL
DEVELOPMENTS IN EAST AND WEST

We have seen how from the very Early Church, Baptism, Confirmation, and the Holy Eucharist formed one continuous rite of Christian Initiation. They were always administered all together at the same Mass as integrated parts of one continuous rite. Furthermore, the bishop of the diocese was the normal celebrant of Baptism and Confirmation, as he was of the Eucharist. However, with time, due to factors like the expansion of the diocese, an increase of rural parishes, a continuing number of infant baptisms throughout the year, and the fear of persecution, it became impossible for the bishop to be the celebrant of every Mass with the Rite of Christian Initiation. As a result, almost everywhere, the parish priest replaced the bishop as the celebrant of the Eucharistic Liturgy. Regarding the Rite of Christian Initiation, however, two divergent trends emerged.

In the East, they wished to preserve the unity of Christian Initiation in one rite. As a result, to this day in the Eastern Churches, Catholic and Orthodox, the priest is the usual minister of the Rite of Christian Initiation, administering Baptism, Confirmation, and Holy Eucharist at the same Mass, even to infants. The traditional authority of the bishop is still present, however, from the fact that the priest can only confirm with the "myron" consecrated by the bishop.

In the West, the desire was to reserve the administration of the sacrament of Confirmation to the bishop. So

Baptism and Confirmation were separated as one continuous rite. The parish priest performed the Baptism. When the bishop was available, he "completed" the Christian Initiation by administering Confirmation by the "laying on of hands" and the anointing with the sacred chrism, as we have already seen.[1]

Further Developments in the West

Gradually, all three elements of Christian Initiation—Baptism, Confirmation, and the Holy Eucharist—became separated into three distinct sacramental ministrations. In fact, in Western practice, these three sacraments began to occur at a different age and stage of Christian development. Baptism, the first act of Christian Initiation, was generally received as an infant. The Eucharist, the goal as well as the ongoing means toward growth and maturity in the Catholic Faith, was generally received at the age of reason. Confirmation, which completed and perfected Baptism, was received at a later age, usually around puberty or early adolescence. This

---

1   It should be mentioned that when the priest baptized the person, an anointing of the newly baptized was performed by the priest with sacred chrism. This was not the sacrament of Confirmation, which was reserved to the bishop. This anointing signified that the newly baptized person now shared in the prophetic, priestly, and kingly offices of Christ. This development in the West began originally in Rome and in those parts of Italy under the direct supervision of the Pope. Later on in the Middle Ages, this practice spread to all of Western Europe and is now the practice of the whole Latin Rite for those baptized as infants. In the case of those baptized as adults, the original continuous Rite of Christian Initiation is now used, as at the Easter Vigil.

development ended up changing the original order of Christian Initiation.[2]

THE EFFECTS OF CONFIRMATION

There are many wonderful effects that come about through the reception of the sacrament of Confirmation. Let us begin by quoting the teaching found in the *Catechism of the Catholic Church*:

> It is evident from its celebration that the effect of the sacrament of Confirmation is the full outpouring of the Holy Spirit as once granted to the Apostles on the day of Pentecost. (#1302)

From this fact, Confirmation brings an increase and deepening of baptismal grace:

- it roots us more deeply in the divine filiation, which makes us cry, "Abba! Father!" (Romans 8:15);
- it unites us more firmly to Christ;
- it increases the gifts of the Holy Spirit in us;

---

2 At the time of the Second Vatican Council, which directed that the rites of all the sacraments be revised to make their meaning clearer to people today, there was discussion of whether we should go back in the West to the original practice of the Church regarding Christian Initiation. There was also a great deal of discussion about the age at which Confirmation should be received. Some wanted it to be for infants, while others wanted the age to be raised even further to stress that Confirmation is the sacrament which, bestowing the Holy Spirit anew upon us, makes us adult Christians, capable of living our spiritual lives more maturely.

- it renders our bond with the Church more perfect (cf. *Lumen Gentium* 11);
- it gives us a special strength of the Holy Spirit to spread and defend the Faith by word and action as true witnesses of Christ, to confess the name of Christ boldly, and never to be ashamed of the Cross (cf. Council of Florence [1439]; DS 1319; *Lumen gentium* 11, 12). (# 1303)

All of these effects are extremely important, but the last effect of a "special strength" and what it enables us to do in our Christian lives closely links us to the role of the Advocate. We shall see in later chapters how the Spirit of Truth assists us to spread or proclaim the Faith, as well as defend it when necessary.

CONTRASTING THE GENERAL EFFECTS OF BAPTISM AND CONFIRMATION

Let us reflect on a few other effects of Confirmation to see how they differ from those of Baptism, since both of these sacraments give us the Holy Spirit.

How each sacrament affects our Christian lives

Baptism is like our spiritual birth, since Jesus describes it as "being begotten of water and Spirit" (John 3:5). By this first outpouring of the Holy Spirit, we are made Christians by the gift of God's life (called Sanctifying Grace) in our souls.

Confirmation is a second outpouring of the Holy Spirit, which perfects or matures our Christian lives by making us grow to spiritual adulthood. It renders us more capable of bearing witness to Jesus, and of confessing and defending our Catholic Faith.

This Christian adulthood brings with it certain new obligations and challenges. First, we should strive to grow spiritually by a more mature and generous practice of the virtues of Christian life, and a more sincere and consistent prayer life. As we just saw, the *Catechism* indicates as effects of Confirmation that we recognize and live out our status as children of God ("divine filiation") with a confident prayer of "Abba! Father!" inspired in our hearts by the Holy Spirit (cf. Romans 8:15). We are also rooted more firmly to Christ, states the *Catechism*. This should make us love Him more genuinely and strive to imitate Him more closely. At the same time, we should work to remove from our lives the obstacles of sin and sinful attachment which hold us back from being open and docile to the guidance and inspirations of the Holy Spirit. This is very important, for as we have seen, the *Catechism* tells us that Confirmation increases the power and effectiveness of the gifts of the Holy Spirit working within us. The Holy Spirit enables us to live the maturity of our Christian adulthood—always, of course, presuming the reception of the sacraments, prayer, and the guidance of the Catholic Church's teachings.

How each sacrament reproduces in us the Mysteries of Christ

By Baptism, the Holy Spirit reproduces in us the "Paschal Mystery" of Christ's death and resurrection. We first die to sin (Original Sin, and any actual sins that may be present in the case of adults) in our Baptism, sharing mysteriously in Jesus' dying on the cross. Then we come to a new life in Christ, sharing the eternal life He won for us by His glorious resurrection.

By Confirmation, the Holy Spirit reproduces in us the event of Pentecost. This was the primary effect of Confirmation mentioned in the *Catechism*, as we have seen above. This second infusion of the Holy Spirit fills us with a prophetic grace, enabling us to become more fully involved in the mission of the Church in proclaiming Christ everywhere and for all times.

Confirmation Imprints a "Character" or "Seal" on the Soul

This effect comes about because, like Baptism, Confirmation imprints on the soul what we call a "character" or "seal," as we have seen above, which is an "indelible spiritual mark." Because it is indelible, this sacrament can never be received again, nor can this mark ever be lost, even by grave sin or apostasy from the Catholic Church. It will remain on the soul forever, adding to the joy and glory of the saints and the humiliation and suffering of the damned. The *Catechism of the Catholic Church* gives us this description of the "character":

> [It] is the sign that Jesus Christ has marked a Christian with the seal of His Spirit by clothing him with power from on high so that he may be His witness (cf. Council of Trent [1547]: DS 1609; Luke 24:48-49). (#1304)

This "character" perfects the common Priesthood of the Faithful; received in Baptism (as distinct from the ordained

Ministerial Priesthood of the clergy received in Holy Orders), and the confirmed person receives the power to profess faith in Christ publicly and as it were officially (*quasi ex officio*) (St. Thomas Aquinas, *Summa Theologica* III, 72, 5, ad 2). (#1305)

This "character," then, gives rise to new obligations for us when we are confirmed. First, we must exercise this "character" or power by participating more actively and intelligently in the Church's Liturgy, something that certainly befits a mature Christian life. At the same time, bonded more closely to the Church (as we have seen above, the *Catechism* stated that this was an effect of Confirmation), we must increase our active participation in the Church's lay ministries and apostolic works of charity and mercy, according to our ability.

Most of all, as we have just seen, the "character" of Confirmation gives us an increased responsibility to "profess faith in Christ publicly and as it were officially." This means living our Catholic Faith as loyal witnesses to Christ. This increased responsibility of Christian witness should likewise motivate us to acquire a mature understanding of our Catholic Faith through reading, instruction, and study.[3] Finally, it also

---

3   This is one of the reasons why the reception of Confirmation is always preceded by a year or two of special review of the Catholic Faith. This is also why the bishop at the Confirmation mass always questions those about to be confirmed. His purpose is to determine: Do they know their Faith, so as to be ready to share it with others and to defend it when it is attacked? As we shall treat in the following chapters, it is the role of the Advocate to help us overcome ignorance, correct errors, and refute falsehood, both for ourselves personally, as well as in dealing with others.

means spreading and defending the Faith boldly and even in the face of opposition and danger of persecution. As we shall see, the Holy Spirit will give us the courage to do this.

THE "SPECIAL STRENGTH" OF CONFIRMATION

A constant tradition, dating all the way back to Tertullian (d. 222) and St. Augustine (d. 430), attributes to Confirmation a grace of "special strength." This strength was especially for bearing witness to Jesus and for spiritual combat to defend the truths He teaches us through His Catholic Church. By the year 800 AD, this tradition was prominent in the West.[4] The sacrament of Confirmation was seen as arming the newly confirmed with the office and responsibility of a soldier of Christ and a defender and promoter of the Faith. This concept of being a "soldier of Christ" is an ancient one, going all the way back to St. Paul who said we must "fight the good fight of Faith" (1 Timothy 6:12). The "desert fathers" (called *abbas*) and the "desert mothers" (called *ammas*) saw themselves as engaged in a relentless spiritual warfare. Nearer to our own time, St. Thérèse of Lisieux wrote in her autobiography, *The Story of a Soul*, that she wanted to be a "warrior for God" fighting on the battlefield of Faith for the cause of Jesus!

Each sacrament is believed to give the recipient a special "sacramental grace" that helps the person to achieve the

---

4   The Council of Florence (1439 AD) was the first ecumenical council to mention Confirmation's special strength for battle in a Church document.

specific purpose of that sacrament. For example, Matrimony gives the married couple the right to those special graces that will help them live good and holy married lives, as well as deal with any difficulties that may arise in their marriage. The special "sacramental grace" of Confirmation is the grace of fortitude or courage. In bearing witness to Jesus, the Spirit of Truth gives those confirmed a special help to live faithful Christian lives in the midst of the many temptations in today's society. They must participate more fully and actively in the Church's mission of redemption, sharing as much as they can in the Church's works of mercy toward those in spiritual and material need. Furthermore, they must confess the name of Jesus boldly and not be ashamed of His cross, even when this is not popular or may cost them in various ways. Finally, some may even be called upon to offer the ultimate witness to Jesus, which is to endure suffering and death for His sake. This is the supreme grace of being a "martyr," to lay down our lives out of the surpassing love of Our Lord, Jesus Christ![5]

St. Ambrose (d. 397), a great bishop and Doctor of the Church, gives us a stirring thought with which to end this chapter on Confirmation:

> Recall then that you have received the spiritual seal, the Spirit of wisdom and understanding, the Spirit of right judgment and courage, the

---

5   It was to remind us to be ready to suffer for Christ that in the old rite of Confirmation before Vatican Council II, the confirming bishop gave each person a slight slap on the cheek!

Spirit of knowledge and reverence, the Spirit of holy fear in God's presence. Guard what you have received. God the Father has marked you with His sign; Christ the Lord has confirmed you and has placed His pledge, the Spirit, in your hearts (De Mys. 7,42; PL 16, 402-403). (See *Catechism of the Catholic Church*, #1303, p. 330)

REFLECTION QUESTIONS

1. The person who receives the Sacrament of Confirmation receives the seal or the mark of the Holy Spirit. Receiving this seal means that you are Christ's. Ponder this for a moment. What does belonging to Christ mean to you?

2. The character of Confirmation gives us an increased responsibility to profess faith in Christ publicly and officially. Do you demonstrate this "public witness" in your life? In what ways?

3. Do you understand the seriousness of your responsibility to study the Faith? Do you take time every day to study it? If you answered yes, how often and consistently do you do so? If you answered no, what practical steps might you take to begin?

4. Have you ever listened to a fellow Catholic successfully defend some aspect of the faith? How did it make you feel? Do you study the faith so that you might also one day be able to defend your faith successfully in the face of opposition?

5. A person who has received the grace of the Sacrament of Confirmation must never be ashamed of the cross, even when it's not popular or may cost him in various ways. Have you ever been ashamed of the cross?

Holy Spirit, powerful Consoler, sacred Bond of the Father and the Son, Hope of the afflicted, descend into my heart and establish in it your loving dominion. Enkindle in my tepid soul the fire of your Love so that I may be wholly subject to you. We believe that when you dwell in us, you also prepare a dwelling for the Father and the Son. Deign, therefore, to come to me, Consoler of abandoned souls, and Protector of the needy. Help the afflicted, strengthen the weak, and support the wavering. Come and purify me. Let no evil desire take possession of me. You love the humble and resist the proud. Come to me, glory of the living, and hope of the dying. Lead me by your grace that I may always be pleasing to you. Amen.

—ST. AUGUSTINE OF HIPPO

CHAPTER 5

THE ADVOCATE DISPELS IGNORANCE

Therefore let us repent and pass from ignorance to knowledge, from foolishness to wisdom, from licentiousness to self-control, from injustice to righteousness, from godlessness to God.

—St. Clement of Alexandria

SACRED SCRIPTURE TELLS US that our first parents, Adam and Eve, enjoyed a great knowledge of things without any need to study to acquire this knowledge. For example, Adam named all the animals (cf. Genesis 2:19-20), yet he never studied zoology. Theologians have traditionally taught that they enjoyed a gift called "infused knowledge." By this gift, God gave directly to their minds a certain knowledge about the things of nature and of human wisdom. This was necessary for them so that they could live their adult lives properly, since there was no one else to teach them the basics of human living. God also infused directly into their minds a knowledge of Himself (remember, they never studied Theology!) so that they could relate to Him properly, using their intelligence to know Him, and their free will to love and serve Him.

However, because of Original Sin, our first parents lost this gift of "infused knowledge" for themselves, as well as for all their descendants. We know the consequences of this loss only too well. We now must learn by studying, which demands hard work and even sacrifice. We can also learn from the trials and tribulations, successes and failures of experience, otherwise known as the "school of hard knocks"! And what are the results of all this effort and pain? It's what I like to call "confused knowledge" because it is a knowledge characterized by gaps of ignorance, mistakes from errors made sincerely, and distortions coming from deliberate falsehood.

Our Heavenly Father, in view of the redemptive victory won for us by Jesus' Death, Resurrection, and Ascension into glory, has sent us the Advocate, the Spirit of Truth, to assist us in healing these wounds of ignorance, error, and falsehood caused by Original Sin. The Advocate does this in a variety of ways, as we shall see. In this chapter, let us focus on the question of ignorance; in the following chapters, we shall deal with error and falsehood.

What Is 'Ignorance'?

In general, ignorance means a lack of the knowledge of something. It can apply to our knowledge in general, but here we shall apply it to the lack of knowledge of our Catholic Faith in particular. Now, not all ignorance is the same. It can have different causes and effects. Therefore, we can distinguish different kinds of ignorance. First, we will view ignorance in terms of whether it is harmful or not to our life of Faith. This will give us the distinction between what we can call "harmless" and "harmful" ignorance. Then we will look at ignorance in terms of whether we are responsible for our ignorance or not. Accordingly, we will distinguish "inculpable" from "culpable" ignorance. These types of ignorance will help us understand more clearly the important role of the Holy Spirit in helping us to dispel ignorance of our Faith.

HARMLESS AND HARMFUL IGNORANCE

Harmless Ignorance

First, we must acknowledge that there is an ignorance that is basically unavoidable for all of us, but one which generally does not cause us harm. There are many areas of human life where we all have to admit ignorance. No scientist, for example, can be an expert in every field of science. Nor can a doctor be a specialist in every field of medicine. The relevant subject matter is too vast for one individual to comprehend everything. This is due to the limitations of human nature. No matter how intellectually gifted, no matter how broad the range of one's study or experience, no matter how long one's life span, there will necessarily always be limits to one's opportunities and one's capacity to learn more. Consequently, everyone will lack the knowledge of many things in life. After all, only God can know all possible things! This unavoidable ignorance, however, usually does no harm to anyone. A person is not responsible for what he or she simply cannot possibly come to know.

Now, if we apply this kind of ignorance to the knowledge of our Catholic Faith, we have to admit that there are areas which learned theologians with post-graduate degrees as well as lay persons trained only in Catholic elementary or secondary schools or CCD programs know little or nothing about. It is necessary that the Church have experts or specialists trained in various fields of the knowledge of our Faith. Examples of these specialists would be Scripture scholars, Canon lawyers, or Church historians. Furthermore, we need clergy and religious who are well-educated, as well as laity properly educated at the college and graduate levels, to carry on effectively the Church's mission of evangelization today.

But just as individuals cannot be experts in every field of human science and endeavor, we cannot expect that every Catholic will be a moral or dogmatic theologian. The knowledge of theology to such a degree goes far beyond the demands or ordinary needs of most Catholics. The lack of knowledge about many minor facts in Church history or very obscure points of theology, for instance, generally does not harm our spiritual growth. If we face a problem for which we need instruction or advice, we can try to find someone with the proper background to answer our questions or solve our difficulties.[1]

---

1 St. Teresa of Avila, quite knowledgeable in mystical theology and prayer, especially through her own experience, had the greatest admiration for theologians who could teach her sound doctrine. She frequently had recourse to them for explanations about points of theology she did not understand, or for counsel regarding problems she was facing.

Harmful Ignorance

There is a second kind of ignorance in life, one that we must be very careful to avoid because it can cause us or others serious harm. It is the lack of required knowledge we expect a person to have in a certain field or on a given topic. This is the case in which we assume that a person who has a responsibility or obligation to know better actually does not. He or she lacks required knowledge. A few examples will illustrate this point. A general medical doctor may not be required to know all the intricacies of bone surgery. He or she, however, is expected to know all the common signs of severe heart trouble. An expectant mother need not be a registered nurse, but she should have a basic knowledge of the proper prenatal and postnatal care of her child.

If we apply this second kind of ignorance to the truths of our Catholic Faith, it would mean that we lack an appropriate knowledge, understanding and appreciation of the basic teachings of our Church. Again, let us look at some examples. A parish priest may not be required to be as fluent in biblical Hebrew as a Scripture scholar, but he should certainly be able to know the differences between the writings of Isaiah the Prophet and St. Paul the Apostle. Ordinary lay persons are not required to be theologians or religious experts, but they should know the Ten Commandments and what they require of all of us, as well as their fundamental Christian responsibilities according to their vocation in life. Without such basic knowledge, we would certainly be harming ourselves spiritually. We would be running the risk of distancing ourselves morally from the Lord. Likewise, if we lack all familiarity with the inspired Word of God in Sacred Scripture, or have no knowledge of prayer, nor of the working of the sacraments in our lives, nor of the meaning of the basic Christian virtues, such ignorance would hold back our necessary growth in holiness. We would not know how to grow spiritually. We might not even be aware that such growth is possible and necessary.

How Can We Overcome Harmful Ignorance?

We can overcome this harmful ignorance in two ways: through the study of our Catholic Faith, and through the gifts of the Holy Spirit. These two means actually work together; one complements the other. The study of our Faith occurs on the external or visible level, while the illumination of the Holy Spirit occurs on the internal or unseen level.

We must not make the mistake of thinking that the gifts of the Holy Spirit, such as Knowledge and Understanding, automatically supply us with a factual knowledge of the teachings of the Church. In other words, the gifts of the Holy Spirit are not the same as "infused knowledge," a knowledge directly poured into our minds by God without any study or effort to learn on our part. Actually, God allows our faith to grow and mature in a very human way. How do we learn other things? We learn when others teach us, and when we study.[2] Once we have learned the basic truths of our Faith, then the gifts of the Holy Spirit work internally on these truths, illuminating and enlightening them. As a result, we better understand and more fully grasp what we have already been taught.

A perfect example of the working of the Holy Spirit is given in the Acts of the Apostles. The episode involves the Deacon Philip and an Ethiopian court official who had gone to Jerusalem on a pilgrimage and was now returning home:

> He (the Ethiopian official) was sitting in his chariot, reading the prophet Isaiah. So the Spirit told Philip, "Go, catch up with that chariot." Now when Philip ran up he heard the man reading from the prophet Isaiah, and he said to him, "Do you understand what you are reading?" "How can I," the man replied, "unless someone explains it to me?" And he urged Philip to get in and sit with him. Now this was the passage of Scripture

---

2 When I was studying philosophy years ago, we used to refer to the mind at birth as a *tabula rasa*, a Latin expression that meant a "blank sheet." In other words, the mind of itself is empty, like a clear sheet of paper. It requires information or data to be fed to it through the senses—through what we see, hear, touch, and experience through all the other senses. If there were no data being fed into the mind through the senses, the mind would have nothing upon which to reflect. The mind needs this raw material from the senses to begin its work of reflection, formation of judgment, and development of deeper understanding. In a similar way, we need to study the basic truths of our Faith through various forms of instruction. The Holy Spirit will then enlighten us further about these basic truths.

he was reading: "He was led like a sheep to the slaughter, and as a lamb is silent before its shearers, He opened not His mouth. He was humiliated and justice was denied Him. Who will ever tell of His posterity, for His life on earth is cut off?" In response the eunuch said to Philip, "Please tell me, who is the prophet referring to, himself or someone else?" Philip opened his mouth and began telling him the good news about Jesus, starting with that very passage of Scripture. As they continued down the road they came to some water, and the eunuch said, "Look, here is some water! What is to keep me from being baptized?" He ordered the chariot to halt and the two of them went down to the water—both Philip and the eunuch—and Philip baptized him. But when they came out of the water, the Spirit of the Lord snatched Philip away and the eunuch saw him no more. He nevertheless went on his way rejoicing. (Acts 8:28-39)

Both the teaching of Philip and the enlightenment of the Holy Spirit were necessary for the Ethiopian official to come to understand the truth about Jesus. Philip first had to instruct the Ethiopian about Jesus. starting with what the prophet Isaiah had written. Then the Spirit enlightened the mind of the court official and opened his heart to receive the message of Philip so that he came to believe and then to request Baptism. We, too, must study our Faith if we are to grow in knowledge of it. In this way, the Holy Spirit with His gifts can help us eliminate any ignorance of the basic doctrines of our Faith that we should all know.

CHRISTIAN INSTRUCTION

"Kerygma" or "Preaching"

The early Christians had two phases or levels of religious instruction. They were known by two Greek words, *kerygma* and *didache*. *Kerygma* referred to a simple proclamation or preaching of the essential truths of our Catholic Faith. This was the primary level of instruction that the Church directed to potential converts as well as to those newly converted. *Kerygma* provided these beginners in the Faith with the fundamental truths about Jesus, the Church, and the meaning of salvation.

Just as the Deacon Philip explained the scriptural passage to the court official and then moved on to tell him briefly the basic message of "the good news of Jesus" (cf. Acts 8:35), we, too, must begin by learning the fundamental truths of our Catholic Faith. For adult Catholics, this *kerygma* is comparable to the primary instructions in the Faith we received as young children either from a family member or friend, or during our early years in a Catholic school or CCD setting. These instructions introduced us to the doctrines and practices of the Church summarized in our "creeds" such as the Apostles' Creed and the Nicene Creed.

"Didache" or "Teaching"

As we mature, we experience a need to move beyond the simple grasp of these basic facts to a deeper knowledge and appreciation of our Faith. We are ready to move from *kerygma* to *didache*. *Didache* referred to a more in-depth teaching. It was directed toward one who was ready to advance in the education and practice of his or her Faith. It involved a more profound study of the Catholic Faith, leading to a more mature understanding of the teachings of the Church and an adult appreciation and love for them.[3]

"Faith Seeks Understanding"

St. Anselm, Archbishop of Canterbury, England, and a Doctor of the Church (AD 1033-1109), taught a very important theological principle: "Faith seeks understanding." What this means is that when we are first introduced to the mysteries of our Faith, for example, as a child or as a potential convert, we usually do not have the intellectual ability or religious background to grasp these beliefs thoroughly. We have to accept them "on faith" in the beginning because we do not yet understand them. To accept something "on faith" is to

---

3   St. Paul prayed earnestly for such maturity of understanding for his converts at Philippi:

> My prayer is that your love may increase more and more, both in understanding and wealth of experience, so that with a clear conscience and blameless conduct you may learn to value the things that really matter, up to the very day of Christ. (Philippians 1:9-10)

accept it on the word of another person. This other person must be someone whom we trust has both the intelligence and the honesty to convince us that what he or she is telling us is the truth and not in any way a deception.

As Catholics, we take the truths of our Faith, first of all, on the word of Jesus, Our Lord, Who revealed these truths to us. Our Lord, as the God-Man, both knows all that He has revealed to us and tells us only what is true. He could never be in error about the truth, nor could He or would He ever deceive us. But our Catholic Faith rests also upon the authority of the Church, especially upon the teaching authority or "Magisterium"[4] of the pope and bishops as the successors of St. Peter and the Apostles. Our Lord clearly gave this teaching authority to His Apostles and through them to His Church when He told them to go and teach all nations (cf. Matthew 28:16-20). He assured His disciples that:

> He who hears you, hears Me. He who rejects you, rejects Me. And he who rejects Me, rejects Him Who sent Me. (Luke 10:16)

The Church has been given both the authority and the responsibility to teach in Jesus' Name. So, when we believe—that is, when our mind gives its "assent of Faith"—our belief rests on two factors: first, that God has revealed these truths, and second, that the Catholic Church authentically teaches them.

---

4   Magisterium is from the Latin word, *magister* = a teacher. It refers to the teaching office Jesus gave to St. Peter and the other Apostles, and which continues now through their successors, the pope and the bishops, teaching in union with him.

These two aspects cannot be separated; one actually guarantees the other. Since God revealed certain truths, His Church must faithfully teach them. On the other hand, since the Catholic Church is unfailingly guided by the Holy Spirit, whatever She officially teaches must be some truth revealed by God or connected with His revealed truths. This is why we have always traditionally prayed at the end of our *Act of Faith*:

> I believe these and all the truths which the Holy Catholic Church teaches, because You, O God, have revealed them, Who can neither deceive nor be deceived.

Thus we begin by believing in these basic truths through faith. St. Paul reminds us that faith is precisely belief in or conviction about the things we do not see (cf. Hebrews 11:1). But then our mind naturally reflects on these truths, analyzes and clarifies them, so as to penetrate more deeply into their meaning and importance for us. In other words, once we accept these teachings as true—because of our faith in them—we are then naturally led to want to understand them more fully. In this way, our faith is seeking greater understanding.

The Example of St. Peter's Faith

A scriptural example may help illustrate this point. Take our Catholic belief in the Holy Eucharist as being Jesus' real Body and Blood[5] and not just a symbol of them. We believe

---

5   Our Catholic belief is that in the Eucharist, Jesus is fully present in His Body, Blood, Soul, and Divinity, for He is truly God (Divinity) and Man (Body, Blood, and Soul).

that the Eucharist is Jesus' "Real Presence." When Our Lord told the crowds (cf. John 6:48-71) that He was the true Bread of Life that had come down from Heaven, and that He would give them His very Body to eat and His very Blood to drink, many people in the crowd objected strenuously to His teaching. They most likely misunderstood this teaching in terms of some kind of cannibalism, and this they found understandably repulsive. But as Jesus insisted on His teaching, the great majority of the crowd walked away from Him (cf. John 6:66) because they did not know how Jesus could do this (cf. Jn 6:52-60). They had falsely assumed Jesus was speaking about some form of cannibalistic ritual. Basically, they did not understand Him, so they rejected Him and His teaching.

Interestingly, Our Lord then turned to His own Apostles and asked them whether they would stay or leave. St. Peter, always reflecting the belief of the little group of Jesus' disciples, responded for all when he said:

> Lord, to whom shall we go? You have the words of eternal life. We have come to believe; we are convinced that You are God's Holy One. (John 6:68-69)

Note the contrast between the crowd that walked away and St. Peter who stayed. The crowd, because they could not understand what Jesus was telling them, would put no trust in Him nor any faith in His teaching. They tried to "understand" before they even "believed" or had faith! No wonder they walked away!

St. Peter, in contrast, had "faith" in Jesus; he was convinced that Jesus taught what He knew to be true, and that He could be believed because He would not deceive anyone. Now, because he believed or trusted in Jesus, St. Peter also accepted "on faith" Jesus' teaching about the Eucharist. Most likely at this point St. Peter, like the crowd, did not intellectually understand how Jesus would give us His Body and Blood to eat and drink, but he believed that if Jesus said He would do it, He would. He was convinced that Jesus' teaching contained "the words of eternal life." Later on, after Jesus instituted the Eucharist at the Last Supper, St. Peter came to "understand" more fully what he had already accepted as true on simple faith. We can only assume that his own personal "devotion" to the Eucharist made him appreciate and love this sacred Bread of Life even more as time went on. Thus, St. Peter's "faith" led him to "understand," whereas the crowd's demand to "understand" first kept them from "faith," from believing at all. Faith operates on the principle that "first you have to believe (have faith) before you can see (understand)," rather than on the principle that "seeing (understanding) is believing (having faith)."

Another similar principle in theology puts it this way: "I believe in order that I may understand."[6] Believing gives us

---

6 This theological principle is also attributed to St. Anselm of Canterbury. He used it in his reflections on proving the existence of God. He wanted to show how the human mind with its power of reasoning (= understanding) can help us more clearly grasp the meaning of those truths we already accept on faith (= believing). His full principle reads: "I do not seek to understand in order that I may believe, but I believe in order that I may understand." St. Anselm made it particularly clear that his attempt to prove God's existence (by reasoning) could not even begin unless he had already believed in His existence (by faith). As he put it: "I desire only a little understanding (in my mind) of the truth which my heart (already) believes and loves."

the time and the opportunity needed to grow in understanding the truths we first accept on faith. This is the very purpose for *didache* or teaching, namely, to educate us in the truths of our Catholic Faith to the point where we can more fully grasp them. The Spirit of Truth is at work here guiding this whole educational process. He is casting His interior light on the truths that we already believe and that we are now studying and reflecting on so that we can better appreciate their spiritual riches for our daily Christian lives. This is the Spirit's gift of "Understanding" at work in us. We certainly need this gift so that we can continue to learn about our Faith as we go through life.

Most Catholics Need a Deeper Knowledge of Their Faith

Many years ago I came across a disturbing fact. It was estimated that the average Catholic in the United States had a seventh grade level of understanding of his or her Faith. This estimate was based on the fact that most Catholic adults had received their Confirmation during the seventh grade and that many of them had afterward discontinued any formal training in their Faith. What a discouraging situation! How far do you think a person would get in the business world today with a seventh grade education?

So we need to study our Faith more deeply. How can we do this? Today, we generally have many resources for education and study available to us. Adults can often find it now through Bible study groups, or the RCIA program, or classes on various religious or spiritual topics in their own local parish or neighboring ones. Some, if they are willing and able, may even want to take classes in a school of theology on a diocesan level. In addition to classes and discussion groups, there are many "self-help" forms of study about our Faith. There are many good books, both classic and contemporary, that can feed our spiritual lives. A top priority should be a mature study of the new *Catechism of the Catholic Church*, preferably with a group and a solid guide to teach and to lead discussions. Also popular today are the use of audio and video tapes that provide us with the opportunity to learn when we have moments of quiet and relaxation. To these means we could add the importance of an occasional good retreat which can challenge us to grow. All of these means are becoming more and more available not only to clergy and religious, but also to the vast number of laity who hunger and thirst for holiness.

Once we find the knowledge of our Faith increasing through our studies, we must pray that the Spirit of Truth will move in us and enable us to see its beauty ever more clearly, and to realize its importance for living our daily Christian lives. It is the Holy Spirit's role to help us appreciate the gift of Faith we have received and to move us to live that Faith with greater understanding, love, and dedication.

INCULPABLE AND CULPABLE IGNORANCE

"Inculpable" Ignorance

There is another aspect about ignorance that merits discussion. This distinction comes from asking ourselves, "Are we responsible for our ignorance?" If we say "no," our ignorance would be called "inculpable" ignorance. If we say "yes," our ignorance is called "culpable." "Inculpable" means "not through my own fault." Many Catholics are ignorant or unaware of their Faith and its demands, but this is not due to any fault or conscious neglect on their part. As a result of this, such a person may do things that actually go against what is required of him or her as a Catholic, or they may omit doing things they should be doing. But because the person does not know any better, he is unaware of the wrong he is doing or the good he is failing to do. In such a case, he would not be guilty of any personal sin to the degree that he is not conscious of his moral obligations.

Two examples of this "inculpable ignorance" will illustrate the point more clearly. A person who does not know that Catholics[7] on Ash Wednesday and Good Friday are still obliged both to fast and to abstain from eating meat does not sin when he goes against these moral obligations if he is unaware of them. Or a person who does not attend Mass on a Holy Day of Obligation because he totally forgets on that day

---

7   The practice of the Catholic Church for both Ash Wednesday and Good Friday is found in Canon 1251 of Canon Law, which reads in part: "Abstinence and fasting are to be observed on Ash Wednesday and Good Friday." Abstinence means not eating meat and fasting means one full meal is allowed, and the other two meals taken together should not equal another full meal.

Canon 1252 indicates the ages of these two obligations: "The law of abstinence binds those who have completed their fourteenth year (= 14 years old). The law of fasting binds those who have attained their majority (= 18 years old), until the beginning of their sixtieth year (= 59 years old)."

is not guilty of any sin. In this sense, the expression, "Ignorance is the eighth sacrament" might well apply.

The Example of St. Paul

St. Paul experienced a kind of inculpable ignorance when he persecuted the early Christians. He really believed he was doing the right thing. He believed Jesus was some kind of an impostor and not the true Messiah. He believed the little Christian movement had to be crushed by persecution so it would not spread further. This all changed when he came to realize the truth along the road to Damascus.

> Now as he traveled along and was approaching Damascus, suddenly a light from the sky shone around him. As he fell to the ground he heard a voice saying to him, "Saul, Saul, why are you persecuting Me?" 'Who are you, Lord?' he asked. The voice answered, "I am Jesus, the One Whom you are persecuting!" (Acts 9:3-5)

Realizing that he was persecuting Jesus in His followers, St. Paul wanted no part of the persecution anymore. Rather, he gave himself completely to the Lord and the service of His Church.

> I give thanks to Jesus Christ our Lord, Who has strengthened me, because by appointing me to this ministry He considered me trustworthy—who had previously been an insolent and blasphemous persecutor. But because I did not know what I was doing in my unbelief, He had mercy on me, and

the grace of our Lord was given to me in abundance, along with the faith and love which are in
Christ Jesus. (1 Timothy 1:12-14)

The great Apostle of the Gentiles was always conscious
of his former way of life as a persecutor of the Church and
lamented the wrong he had done. Yet, he was even more
conscious of God's gracious mercy and favor that chose
him when he was least worthy of His call. (cf. 1 Corinthians
15:9-10)

Sometimes people are tempted to want to remain in such
ignorance. Ignorance can seem to be bliss. Actually, although
such ignorance may occasionally save a person from doing
moral wrong, it generally does not help him do what is morally right. Furthermore, when a person later learns the truth,
he may even regret the wrong he did in his ignorance. For
example, how many women have had abortions sincerely
believing it was not wrong, sincerely believing that it was not
a child whose life they were ending. Later, however, when
they came to realize the true facts, they were crushed by a
great sense of guilt for something they did in their ignorance.

"Culpable" Ignorance

If a person were deliberately to foster such ignorance, it would
then become "culpable" ignorance or ignorance "through
one's own fault." A person who consciously remains in a state
of ignorance even though he knows he can and should learn
more about the Faith and his responsibilities as a Catholic,
not only prevents any further growth in his Faith, but also
runs the risk of offending God. If a person refuses to learn

more about his Faith simply to avoid realizing all his obligations as a Catholic, he actually becomes directly responsible before God for such willful ignorance. The Lord will hold that person accountable for such deliberate ignorance. That person also becomes indirectly responsible for all the wrong deeds he does because of such deliberate ignorance.

Let Us Ask the Advocate to Give Us a Great Hunger for Truth

Let us not fall into a "minimalist" attitude, saying, "I'll give God the least I have to," or "I'll try to get away with the most I can," or "I'll play it as close to the line as I can." God blesses generous and cheerful givers, not those who count every cost and give only begrudgingly the least amount of love and service they feel compelled to give. Ignorance can be like terrible shackles from which the Spirit of Truth wishes to set us free. As Jesus once said, "The truth will set you free" (John 8:32). Let us not allow ourselves to be imprisoned by willful ignorance. Rather, let us ask the Spirit of Truth in humble prayer to open us up to the joy and peace and deep satisfaction that comes from possessing the Truth, since God is Truth! After all, our minds and hearts have been made for God's truth and love. It is for this truth and love that we all long—whether we realize it or not—in the depths of our being!

What we must do is to ask the Holy Spirit in prayer to create in us a "positive hunger" for the truth of the Lord. This truth can be found in both the inspired Word of God in the Sacred Scriptures as well as in the true doctrine of our

Catholic Church as it has come down to us over the centuries through the Magisterium of the Church in Sacred Tradition. It is an important Catholic doctrine that Sacred Tradition and Sacred Scripture both form a unity in transmitting to us the sacred "deposit of faith," the sum total of the truth revealed by Jesus and His Apostles and committed to the care of the Catholic Church for all time.

> "Sacred Tradition and Sacred Scripture, then, are bound closely together and communicate one with the other. For both of them, flowing out from the same divine well-spring, come together in some fashion to form one thing and move towards the same goal" (*Dei Verbum* #9). Each of them makes present and fruitful in the Church the mystery of Christ, Who promised to remain with His own "always, to the close of the age." (Matthew 28:20) (*Catechism of the Catholic Church*, #80, p. 26)

> "Sacred Scripture is the speech of God as it is put down in writing under the breath of the Holy Spirit" (*DV*, #9). "And (Holy) Tradition transmits in its entirety the Word of God which has been entrusted to the apostles by Christ the Lord and the Holy Spirit. It transmits it to the successors of the apostles, mainly, the bishops, so that, enlightened by the Spirit of Truth, they may faithfully preserve, expound and spread it abroad by their preaching" (*DV*, #9). (*Catechism of the Catholic Church*, #81, p. 26)

As a result, the Church, to whom the transmission and interpretation of Revelation is entrusted, "does not derive her certainty about all revealed truths from the holy Scriptures alone. Both Scripture and Tradition must be accepted and honored with equal sentiments of devotion and reverence" (*DV*, #9). (*Catechism of the Catholic Church*, #82. p. 26)

We must ask the Holy Spirit, as mentioned already, to stir up in us a "positive" spiritual hunger for the truth. Not every hunger is "positive" in character. If the hunger is due to deprivation of the truth, this would be quite "negative," even if the person were unaware of what they were being deprived of. It would be tantamount to spiritual starvation. The prophet Amos spoke of such a spiritual famine in his day concerning the Word of God:

Yes, days are coming, says the Lord God, when I will send famine upon the land: not a famine of bread, or thirst for water, but for hearing the Word of the Lord. Then shall they wander from sea to sea and rove from the north to the east in search of the Word of the Lord, but they shall not find it. (Amos 8:11-12)

The spiritual hunger we are to ask for must come from a longing to hear God's Word and to learn the truths of our Catholic Faith. These are what give life and set us free from the ignorance and confusion that characterize the lives of so many people today. Like finding a treasure hidden in a field or a pearl of great price that we have been searching for (cf. Matthew 13:44-46), we must be so desirous of God's truth that no "price"—no effort, no sacrifice—will be too much to pay. The Spirit of Truth will create this hunger in us by His Gifts of Knowledge and Wisdom. By Knowledge, He will let us see the passing vanity and emptiness of earthly pleasures and human prudence. He will also enlighten us to recognize that created things are only good and beneficial if they help us get closer to God. By Wisdom, He will give our minds a taste or relish for the truths of God and for God Himself as the greatest of all treasures. Such a spiritual hunger is, indeed, a powerful cure for ignorance concerning the truth of God!

REFLECTION QUESTIONS

1. Do you consider yourself knowledgeable in the basics of your Catholic Faith (e.g., Ten Commandments, 7 Sacraments, difference between mortal sin versus venial sin, etc.)? What do you do or who do you consult when you have a question about a teaching of the faith?

2. When was the last time you read a spiritual book, listened to a CD, watched a video or participated in a bible study to help you learn more about your faith?

3. Do you read the bible daily? If so, how has it helped you to grow in your faith journey? If not, how might you incorporate this practice into your daily routine?

4. Did you know that a positive spiritual hunger is a very powerful cure for ignorance concerning the truth of

God? Do you ask the Holy Spirit daily, to stir up in you a positive hunger for the truth?

Come, Holy Spirit. Spirit of Truth,
You are the reward of the saints, the
Comforter of souls, light in the darkness,
riches to the poor, treasure to lovers, food
for the hungry, comfort to those who are
wandering; to sum up, You are the One
in Whom all treasures are contained.
Come! As You descended upon Mary
that the Word might become flesh, work
in us through grace as You worked in
her through nature and grace. Come!
Food of every chaste thought, fountain
of all mercy, sum of all purity. Come!
Consume in us whatever prevents us
from being consumed in You.

—ST. MARY MAGDALENE DE PAZZI

CHAPTER 6

THE ADVOCATE
CORRECTS ERRORS

*Error never shows itself in its naked reality, in order not
to be discovered. On the contrary, it dresses elegantly, so
that the unwary may be led to believe that it is more
truthful than truth itself.*

—St. Irenaeus of Lyons

IN THIS CHAPTER I AM USING "error" to mean a sincere mistake about a truth of our Catholic Faith. This presumes that the person is sincere in his mistaken belief and not simply trying to deceive himself. In other words, he does not realize any misrepresentation of the truth on his part, but instead he is really convinced that what he says or believes is the truth.

Errors in regard to our knowledge of the Faith happen frequently, even to those who may know the Catholic Faith well. St. Augustine, for example, shortly before his death wrote two volumes called his *Retractions* in which he revised opinions or corrected teachings he had made in all of his earlier works. This outstanding Father of the Church had a great mind, yet he did not enjoy the privilege of infallibility. He felt the need to revise many of his earlier doctrinal explanations, because he concluded later on that they were erroneous. Compared to this great Doctor of the Church, imagine how frequently we will be mistaken!

What Are the Causes of Such Errors?

Faulty Instruction

Errors can come from various causes. Let us deal with some of them. Errors can be due, first of all, to faulty instruction. No teacher, for example, is perfect. A teacher's own human limitations to understand adequately the teachings of the Catholic Church, or to be able to explain them in a way which is clear to his students, undoubtedly affect the student's grasp of what is taught. Add to this the fact that teachers may have a certain "bias" or prejudice, a "hidden agenda" if you will, that colors or distorts the way they look at official Church teaching, and how they convey that teaching to their students. A teacher might want to promote ideas that are very liberal or somehow stretch or diminish the truth, thereby distorting it. For example, a teacher of Sacred Scripture may tend towards a "rationalistic" view of the Bible and thus deny as historical any events that need a "supernatural" explanation, such as miracle stories. For such teachers, real "miracles" did not actually happen; they were just natural occurrences that people in biblical times could not properly explain or that they embellished for effect. For example, they might say—as did many biblical rationalists in the nineteenth century—that Jesus did not actually walk on the waters of the Sea of Galilee during a storm (cf. Mark 6:45-52). According to them, He was merely floating on a raft or large board, maybe even a surfboard!

In another example, such rationalistic teachers claim that Jesus did not miraculously multiply the five loaves of bread and two fish (cf. John 6:1-13). Had Jesus performed an actual miracle, this would have been a "supernatural" event, and rationalists assume as a starting point that such events did not—in fact, could not—happen. These events must have a simple natural explanation. So, these rationalists claim that when the young boy so generously gave his remaining loaves and fishes to Jesus, all the people hoarding their own personal food felt guilty. In their shame, these people opened up their knapsacks and shared with others what they had been hiding away for themselves. The result of such an explanation is the absolute denial that any real miracle ever took place, even though the Gospel story clearly describes that an actual miracle did occur. A sad consequence of such distorted explanations is that many Catholic students today often are in error in their understanding of the Scriptures and authentic Catholic doctrine in general.

Lack of Necessary Content

Another source of errors regarding the knowledge of our Catholic Faith can be traced to the faulty textbooks used in the religious instruction of our students. Many of them, especially in the years immediately following Vatican Council II, contained little or no content. The emphasis was often on experience at the expense of dogma and doctrine. Students educated with such minimal content very often have many gaps in their religious knowledge. resulting in a faulty knowledge of the Catholic Faith which can be, and too often has been, passed on from one generation to the next. These errors can be corrected as time goes on by further study in a solid religious education program or through good reading.[1]

Resistance to the Truth

Errors often result from a conscious or even an unconscious resistance to the truths being taught. Some persons may not be very open to Church teaching, perhaps because of intellectual difficulties and objections that they are not able to resolve satisfactorily. For others, there is resistance because such teachings would make certain practical demands on their lifestyles that they are presently unwilling to meet.

The widespread rebellion against authority that prevailed in society in the 1960s and 1970s flowed over into the Church. This was seen especially in the reaction to Blessed Pope Paul VI's encyclical, *Humanae Vitae*. This important papal encyclical reiterated the Church's traditional condemnation of artificial birth control while at the same time reaffirming the value and dignity of all human life, even that of the unborn. Many people closed their minds and hearts to this teaching;

---

1   For example, after Vatican II, many of the textbooks used to teach religion to our Catholic youth were criticized for being more concerned with the relevance of ideas than with solid content. They sought to present material that seemed appealing to the students, but frequently at the price of necessary teachings or any real depth of explanations.

open rebellion within the Church against this traditional teaching (as well as many others) became obvious.

When Pope St. John XXIII's encyclical on the Church, *Mater et Magistra* (Mother and Teacher), appeared, some people (especially some very liberal theologians) were saying: "*Mater—Si, Magistra—No*" ("Mother—Yes, Teacher—No"). Translated in reference to the Church, it meant that these people were willing to look to the Church for the support it gave through the sacraments and prayer, to be nourished by her as a mother feeds her children, but they did not want the Church to teach them, to direct them, to spell out for them what the Gospel message entailed. Basically, they rejected the Catholic Church's authority and the teaching role She had been given by the Divine Teacher Himself. They reserved that role to themselves, or to whatever particular philosophical or theological viewpoint they chose to follow.

Besides those who openly rebel against the teaching authority of the Church, there are many others who unconsciously resist it. Perhaps they resist because they do not like clarity. They are much more comfortable with obscure or contentious theological points, points which they feel are still up for discussion, debate, and even private interpretation. If there is no clarity on a given doctrine, then there is no obligation to give it the assent of faith, or to put that teaching into practice. Once clarity is arrived at, then the person would feel a moral obligation to respond and live by that teaching.

Our Knowledge Comes Progressively

Another reason for errors—again, we mean sincere mistakes—is due to the very progressive nature of growth in human knowledge. In this instance, error might better be called a "limited" or "incomplete" grasp of the truth. We have not received "infused knowledge" like the angels who received all their knowledge and understanding from God at once. Rather, we human beings must grow in knowledge by a slow process. It demands study, reflection, and prayer.

Blessed Cardinal Newman once remarked: "To live is to change, and to have lived fully is to have changed often." When it comes to our religious knowledge, we do not change essential truths. This is absolutely important to stress, so as to avoid any serious misunderstanding here. For example, there is and always will be only One God in Three Divine Persons. Furthermore, the Three Divine Persons will always be the Father, the Son, and the Holy Spirit. What will change, however, and in a sense must change, especially over the span of our lifetime, is the way in which we humanly understand Who God is. Any human idea of God is by its very nature limited because the capacity of our human intelligence is limited. Only God can fully know and understand Himself. This is because He is an infinite Being; He alone has the infinite intelligence needed to understand Himself completely.

Our human ideas of God and of how He deals with us, on the other hand, will always be limited. Consequently, they will always be inadequate or insufficient to understand God's infinite being completely. Only God with His infinite intelligence, as we already said, can fully comprehend Himself in His infinite nature all at once. With our limited intelligence, we at best can only faintly grasp God's infiniteness. We do this in a piecemeal manner, a little part at a time! That is why we will go on learning more and more about God in this life. As we learn more about Him, we will have to change or adjust some of our previous ideas about God in order to include our new knowledge of Him. Remember, God does not change. Being infinite, He cannot change. What changes is the way we understand Him!

CORRECTING ERRORS REQUIRES MATURING IN OUR UNDERSTANDING OF GOD

In order to grow in the knowledge of God and His ways so as to arrive at a fuller understanding of Who He is, we must be able to adjust or revise some of our previous ideas of Him. St. Augustine once expressed it this way: "God is more unlike what we think Him to be than He is like what we think Him to be!" Therefore, in order to mature according to our human progressive way of learning, we have to be able to adjust certain concepts or ideas about God and spiritual things that we had growing up, especially some of those from childhood.

Examples of St. Paul

St. Paul himself experienced this same process and expressed it clearly:

> Our knowledge is imperfect and our prophesying is imperfect. When the perfect comes, the imperfect will pass away. When I was a child, I spoke like a child, thought like a child, reasoned like a child. When I became a man, I put aside childish ways. Now we see indistinctly, as in a mirror; then we shall see face to face. My knowledge is

imperfect now; then I shall know even as I am known. (1 Corinthians 13:9-12)

St. Paul recognized the imperfection of human knowledge in regard to understanding God. He clearly saw the need to discard or correct childish notions about God and about the spiritual life. Otherwise these notions become obstacles to further growth in holiness. For example, a person in childhood may naively form the notion that as long as he says his prayers, no difficulties will ever come into his daily life. Yet, obviously, trials and difficulties of all sorts happen even to very good people who say their prayers every day.[2] Such a naive idea could easily prove very detrimental in a person's spiritual life. It would be quite different, of course, to say that as long as one said his prayers faithfully, he can hope that God will always be there to help him through his trials. That is one thing. But to say that trials will never come because a person says his prayers every day, that is quite another matter. There is a need to adjust such a limited or faulty concept in order to deal maturely with the trials that inevitably befall every true Christian.

St. Paul provides us with another example of an erroneous attitude in the spiritual life that often must be corrected. It is a subtle temptation that afflicts many good people. It is the temptation to feel that once we have made some noticeable progress in conquering our main sins and faults or in

---

2   Job in the Old Testament is certainly an outstanding example of this. Our Lady with Her traditional seven sorrows is another example of this in the New Testament. They both suffered great trials despite their extraordinary holiness.

practicing certain virtues, that we do not need to strive much more on the road of spiritual development. The progress we have made can easily lull us into feelings of false pride and security ("I've achieved more than enough virtue!") or into a spiritual sloth ("I don't have to keep trying any more!"). St. Paul points out that in our spiritual striving we must all imitate long distance runners who do not keep looking back over the part of the course they have already covered, but keep their eyes intently focused on the goal line toward which they are running. He mentions that this is the way everyone who grows to maturity in the spiritual life should view the road to holiness. He adds that if we erroneously see it any other way, the Holy Spirit will have to correct us.

> My entire attention is on the finish line as I run toward the prize to which God calls me—life on high in Christ Jesus. Those of us who are spiritually mature must adopt this attitude. If you see it another way, God will clarify the difficulty for you. It is important that we continue on our course, no matter what stage we have reached. (Philippians 3:14-16)

As a spiritual director, I have often found great consolation in this particular quote of St. Paul. It reminds me that when I cannot clarify certain difficulties of those I am directing, God will take care of them in His own good time and in His own good way. St. Paul's main point here is very important: it would be an unfortunate mistake to think that, if we have made some progress on our spiritual journey, that would be enough, and we do not have to go any further.

The apostle wisely points out that just the opposite is true: no matter how much progress we have already made, there is still more to be made. So we must not stop. Many saints and spiritual writers have emphasized this principle, "In the spiritual life, a person never stands still. Not to go forward is to go backward in the spiritual life."

St. Francis' Experience

One other example of God clarifying any misunderstandings we may have of His message is found in the life of St. Francis of Assisi. It deals with an experience he had at the time of his conversion. He had already begun to listen attentively to the Lord calling him to conversion and to his mission in life. St. Bonaventure gives us the following description of a very important event that affected St. Francis' life profoundly:

> Christ Himself was Francis' only guide during all this time and now in His goodness, He intervened once more with the sweet influence of His grace. Francis left the town one day to meditate out of doors, and as he was passing by the Church of San Damiano which was threatening to collapse with age, he felt urged to go in and pray. There as he knelt in prayer before a painted image of the Crucified, he felt greatly comforted in spirit and his eyes were full of tears as he gazed at the Cross. Then, all of a sudden, he heard a voice coming from the Cross and telling him three times, "Francis, go and repair My house. You see it is

all falling down." Francis was alone in the church and he was terrified at the sound of the voice, but the power of its message penetrated his heart and he went into an ecstasy. Eventually, he came back to himself and prepared to obey the command he had received. He was quite willing to devote himself entirely to repairing the ruined church of San Damiano, although the message really referred to the universal Church which Christ ". . . won for Himself at the price of His own Blood" (Acts 20:28), as the Holy Spirit afterwards made him realize and he himself explained to the friars. (*Major Life*, II. par. 1)

In this example, we see that St. Francis at first mistakenly interpreted the message Christ spoke to him. He initially understood it to refer principally—in fact, exclusively—to the task of rebuilding the many dilapidated little chapels that dotted the Assisi countryside. In obedience to Jesus' command as he understood it, he first rebuilt the chapel of San Damiano where Jesus had spoken to him from the cross. When he finished there, he proceeded to rebuild the chapel of San Pietro in honor of St. Peter, the Prince of the Apostles. When that task was completed, he repaired an ancient little chapel in honor of the Virgin Mary called St. Mary of the Angels. This was his favorite chapel of all. However, it was only gradually that his limited understanding was corrected under the influence of the Holy Spirit. The Spirit of Truth made Francis realize that he had been called by Jesus, not to repair little dilapidated stone chapels, but to reform the universal Church, redeemed by the Blood of Christ. He was to rebuild the Church in the hearts of the people by stirring up once again renewed faith in God and generous love for Him by the holiness of his life and by his zealous preaching and work with the poor. St. Francis was led by the light of the Holy Spirit from understanding his life's mission as a very limited physical work of repairing chapels to a very broad spiritual mission of renewing the whole Church.

Areas of Confusion

"Sincerity" versus "Truth"

Before concluding this chapter, there are a few areas of confusion that are worth reflecting upon to offer some clarification. One area is the confusion of "sincerity" with "truth." In today's society, we are very keenly aware and sensitive to the sincerity of people. Sometimes, however, we use the sincerity of a person or the sincerity with which they say something to us as the gauge of the truth of what they are saying. However, sincerity and truth are two very different things. A person can be quite sincere and yet quite wrong at the same time. A little child who says very innocently that two plus two equals five may be beyond reproach as regards his sincerity, for he may really believe it. At the same time, however, since two plus two equals four, the child is in error, no matter how innocent his mistake may be.

A classic illustration in the Bible of the distinction between sincerity and truth is found in the Gospel of

St. Matthew where Jesus puts two questions to His disciples in the area around Caesarea Philippi:

> When Jesus came to the district of Caesarea Philippi, He began to question His disciples: "Who do people say that the Son of Man is?" They replied. "Some say John the Baptizer, others Elijah, still others Jeremiah or one of the prophets." Then He asked them, "But who do you say I am?" Simon Peter replied, "You are the Messiah, the Son of the living God." In response, Jesus said to him, "Blessed are you Simon, son of Jonah! No mere man has revealed this to you but My Father in Heaven." (Matthew 16:13-17)

When Our Lord asked His first question, "Who do people say that the Son of Man is?" He received a lot of nice answers, but they were all wrong answers! Certainly the people were quite sincere when they judged Our Lord mistakenly to be John the Baptist (who had a ministry, a message, and a popularity quite like Jesus' own), or Elijah (who was expected before the end of the world), or Jeremiah (Our Lord was possibly mistaken for Jeremiah because both were celibate and this was a very rare occurrence among the Jews) or a prophet (surely a man favored by God and proclaiming His message). These answers that the people gave regarding Jesus' identity were all very good. After all, who are better people than John the Baptist or Elijah or Jeremiah or the prophets? Yet, despite the sincerity of their answers, all these answers were wrong.

Then, when Our Lord asked the disciples His second question, "Who do you say that I am?", Simon Peter responded, "You are the Messiah, the Son of the Living God." St. Peter, like the people, was also sincere; however, he had one advantage—his answer was also correct. It had been revealed to him by our Heavenly Father through the gift of faith that Jesus was the long-awaited Messiah and even more, He was and is the Son of the Living God!

This distinction between truth and sincerity is very important, and it should always be kept in mind. Truth, as we have already seen, is an "objective" quality. For ideas or words to be "true," they must correspond to what really exists. In the example at Caesarea Philippi, Jesus was really the Messiah and really the Son of the Living God as St. Peter had proclaimed Him to be, and so his understanding and his words concerning Jesus were objectively true. Jesus was not John the Baptist, nor Elijah, nor Jeremiah, nor a simple prophet as the people were thinking and saying—so their thoughts and words were objectively in error.

Sincerity, by contrast, is a "subjective" quality. To be "sincere" people must be basically honest. In other words, people are sincere if they avoid any deliberate lies or distortions of what they believe to be true. However, unless these persons enjoy the gift of "infallibility," there are bound to be times when, no matter how "sincere" they are, they will still be mistaken, as were the people quoted in the Caesarea Philippi story.

Misguided Ecumenism

Another area of confusion or error for many Catholics today has come through association with non-Catholic Christians in certain circumstances that have led these Catholics to adopt particular beliefs that are in conflict with our own Catholic teachings. The ecumenical movement after Vatican Council II has been for Catholics, by and large, a movement of great grace. It has allowed Catholics to recognize in other Christians their separated brothers and sisters in Christ. They have come to realize the importance of working toward that Christian unity for which Jesus prayed and to which He referred when He spoke of Himself as the Good Shepherd of the whole flock:

> I have other sheep who are not of this fold, and I
> must lead them, too. They shall listen to My voice,
> and there shall be one flock then, one shepherd.
> (John 10:16)

I do not mean to say here that confusion comes from good ecumenical prayer, whether in prayer groups or during the "Week of Unity Octave" (January 18-25) when we pray for Church unity. This is the unity Christ Himself prayed for and desired. Nor do I mean here that confusion comes from ecumenical cooperation, out of which a great deal of good has come. For example, ecumenical endeavors in running soup kitchens and shelters for the homeless and the poor, or in combating evils such as pornography, or especially in the defense of the right to life of the unborn, are truly works of the Holy Spirit moving among us. I believe they are helping to move us toward that unity Christ willed for us.

Rather, a great deal of confusion and error has come from so called television and radio evangelism and the fundamentalist literature available today. Many of these media evangelists have a strong anti-Catholic bias. Stressing the Bible only, they disregard the living Tradition that is so much a part of the Catholic Church's 2000 year experience. Because of this, many Catholics have become confused about what they believe, while some have downplayed or even denied many essential areas of Catholic doctrine and practice. For example, the Eucharist is often reduced to a "symbol" and no longer the reality of Christ's Body, Blood, Soul, and Divinity. There has been neglect of Confession because many Catholics are taught to feel "saved" by faith alone. They have been encouraged to drift away from devotion to Our Lady and to the saints, which they are erroneously told take the focus off of Christ. At the same time they end up rejecting certain doctrines, such as that of Purgatory, because they mistakenly are told it cannot be proven in Scripture.[3] It is no wonder that there is confusion and error on the part of many Catholics who have been influenced by such fundamentalist evangelism.

---

3   In reality there is clear evidence in Sacred Scripture of the existence of Purgatory in the Second Book of Maccabees, which Fundamentalists readily omit from the Scriptural Canon or official list of inspired books of the Bible.

Some Ways to Correct Errors

In order to eliminate confusion or to correct erroneous ideas, a person can use a number of means. Certainly, a person would do well to have a sincere talk with a good priest to clarify his or her difficulties. A person could also enroll in a study program on the Faith. A good retreat can once again revive a person's sense of being Catholic. Reading some of the good Catholic literature which is readily available today, especially the *Catechism of the Catholic Church*, will provide a much more mature explanation of Church teaching and practice. Learning some of the history and the development of various devotions in the Church, as well as the background to her doctrinal teachings and rites, makes Catholics appreciate their Faith more personally.

Finally, and most important of all, we must pray to the Spirit of Truth to give us a deeper understanding and love for our Catholic Faith. This increased appreciation will lead to the determination to be loyal to the Church and her truths. This is certainly very, very important. I have worked with people who have either left the Church or at least have come close to leaving the Church because they have been greatly confused about the meaning and teachings of the Church. However, once they returned, or simply corrected certain erroneous ideas and dispelled their confusion, they rekindled their Catholic Faith with renewed enthusiasm and dedication. The Spirit of Truth had even corrected errors they might have been quite unaware of, but that had nevertheless shackled them. The Spirit of Truth had brought them the truth that truly set them free.

REFLECTION QUESTIONS

1. The Church is both Mother and Teacher. Do you whole-heartedly accept and trust the teaching authority of the Church?

2. Do you own a copy of the Catechism of the Catholic Church? Do you refer to it when you have questions about the faith that you need some clarification on? How often have you read it in the last year?

3. What is your attitude towards other people (public officials or close family members and friends) who consider themselves Catholic but hold erroneous views about certain beliefs of the Catholic Church (e.g., on same sex unions, abortion, contraception, etc.) because of their ignorance of the faith? Can you distinguish between the "sincerity" of what they are saying and the "truth" or "error" of their position? Do you pray for them?

4. Have you ever tried to "correct" another person's misunderstanding of a belief of the Catholic Faith? What was the error about and how did you go about making the correction?

5. Do you try to plant seeds in the minds and hearts of your family members and friends who do not understand some of the truths of the Catholic Faith? Besides prayer, what other practical ways do you try to do this?

Divine Guest, Master, Light, Guide, Love,
may I make You truly welcome inside me
and listen to the lessons You teach me.
Make me burn with eagerness for you,
make me follow You and love You.

—ST. JOSEMARÍA ESCRIVÁ
THE FORGE #430

CHAPTER 7

THE ADVOCATE
OPPOSES FALSEHOOD

When lies have been accepted for some time, the truth
always astounds with an air of novelty.

—St. Clement of Alexandria

FALSEHOOD IS A DELIBERATE distortion of the truth. It differs from error since someone in error may act in good faith and may not realize that he is mistaken. Presumably, such a person would be ready to correct the error once he is made aware of it. Errors made in good faith often happen to persons who lack either the ability or the training needed to distinguish right from wrong or truth from non-truth.

Falsehood, on the other hand, implies that a person knowingly distorts the truth or twists the facts. He may do so to discredit the real truth or to make his distorted statement seem "correct" or "obvious." Such a person generally can distinguish right from wrong or fact from fiction, but he chooses not to do so.

Falsehood from outside the Church

Falsehood chiefly comes from outside the Church—from her obvious enemy, the world.[1] The falsehood of the world can come in different ways.

Persecution

One of the main ways is through persecution. Our Lord Himself suffered persecution at the hands of the religious leaders of His day, especially the Pharisees and Scribes. Religious persecution means to harass or oppress people, even to the point of inflicting punishment or injury on them because they hold to their religious beliefs. This happened, for example, for decades in Communist countries where those who believed in Christ—who refused to abandon the truth of Him Who called Himself "the Truth" (cf. John 14:6)—were denied

---

1   Here we must make a very important distinction concerning the meaning of "the world." In St. John's Gospel, sometimes the expression "the world" is used very positively, at other times very negatively. An example of its positive use is to refer to the world as the creation of God, as an object of His love and care. In this sense "the world" is good. In a verse that many people consider to be the most beautiful verse in the whole Bible, "the world" is very much loved by God the Father:

> Yes, God so loved the world that He gave His only Son, that whoever believes in Him may not die but may have eternal life. (John 3:16)

But on the other hand, "the world" can also be used in a very negative sense. It is the word used to describe that spirit which is in opposition to Christ and to His Church. Much falsehood comes from this opposition.

jobs, government benefits, social advancement, as well as the freedom to practice their religion without hindrance.

Deliberate Distortions of Church Teachings

In addition to this pressure put on believers to abandon their faith, there were obvious attempts to distort the truth deliberately. Examples of this include the "rewriting" of history, distorting the facts so as to make the Church and her doctrine seem negative, outdated, even contrary to the best interests of the people. This type of "revisionist" history is not only produced by totalitarian type governments opposed to the Church, such as in former Communist countries, but even by those forces which control the education system in countries which boast of an "openness" and "freedom of education." It can be seen in certain history books mandated for public schools, not only by what they write, but also by what they omit. Many people are misled by these "revisionist" tactics to turn away from the Church or even become prejudiced against it. This is why all Catholics need a good, solid education in the truths of their Catholic Faith, including the history of the Church. There is no substitute for this basis to our Faith. Once we possess this basic education, the Holy Spirit can draw from our knowledge of the truth to help us recognize when the truth is being distorted.

Anti-Religious Censorship

Censorship is another means used to distort the teachings of religion. Censorship prevents religious truths from being communicated, either in full or in part, to believers. It is primarily imposed on those who are charged with the responsibility to teach in the Christian community. Priests' sermons and religious classes, for example, are subjected in certain countries to constant scrutiny, and may be censored or restricted as to content. Textbooks, likewise, may be subject to censorship with the result that necessary content is prohibited and must be omitted or deleted.

Censorship can also mean that any access to the means of public or mass communications, especially by television or radio or even the Internet, may be denied to certain individuals or religious groups, or at least sharply restricted. All of this censorship is done with a view to distorting the Church's doctrine in the minds and hearts of believers by denying them the right to know their Catholic Faith.

Propaganda or "Catholic Bashing"

Another form of falsehood coming from the world is propaganda, better called "Catholic bashing." This is the consistent and deliberate effort to discredit the Catholic Church. We find it is rampant today, especially in the media. Sometimes it exposes the Church's teaching to ridicule and even contempt by misrepresenting it, or presenting it in a bad light, such as an object of cheap laughter in a TV sitcom. At other times, it takes the form of relentlessly exposing either the weaknesses of the Church's members or scandals involving well-known high-ranking members of the Church in a way that they would not treat other religious groups.

"Catholic bashing" in the media has become a serious problem for the Church. Because of the widespread ignorance about the truth of the Church today, many Catholics form their opinion and understanding of their own

Church more from what they see in the media than from what they once studied or are currently experiencing in their own practice of the Faith. As a result, many Catholics have a terribly distorted and confused idea of their own religion. What they have learned is often based on surveys (of many people equally lacking knowledge of the Catholic Faith) or on commentaries by media people, many of whom are not only not Catholic but agnostics or atheists (and so presumably are ignorant of the Catholic Faith) and some of whom have a prejudiced, hostile attitude toward anything Catholic. What chance is there of them ever getting a clear, complete, and unbiased picture of the Catholic Church in the secular media?

I am convinced that many Catholics who leave the Church and either join other religious groups, Christian or non-Christian, or simply give up on organized religion in any form, are doing so because of these distorted views. In many cases, they are not really leaving the Catholic Church as such—they simply do not have the right picture. They are believing a caricature or a distortion. If they knew the real truth of the Church and the true beauty of the Catholic life fully lived, I believe many of them would not leave.

Jesus Foretold the Opposition of the World

The world's attempts to distort the truth of the Church should not in any way surprise us. Jesus clearly foretold it. In a sense, He included this "opposition of the world" into the "contract" He gave us to become His followers. It was there in the bold print, so to speak, from the very beginning. In St. John's Last Supper account Jesus twice refers to the opposition of the world. The first time He tells His Apostles that "the world" would hate them:

> If you find the world hates you, remember that it hated Me before you. If you belonged to the world, the world would love you as its own; the reason it hates you is that you do not belong to the world. But, instead, I chose you from the world. Remember the word I spoke to you; no slave is greater than his master. If they persecuted Me, they will persecute you as well. They will respect your words as much as they respected Mine. All this they will do to you because of My name, because they know nothing of the One Who sent Me. If I had not come and spoken to them, they would not be guilty of sin. Now, however, they have no excuse for their sin. Whoever hates Me also hates My Father. Had I not performed such works among them as no one has ever performed before, they would not be guilty of sin; but as it is, they have seen and still they go on hating Me and My Father. However, this only fulfills the word written in their law: "They hated Me without cause." (John 15:18-25)

Here Our Lord foretells the hatred of the world. The precise reason for this bitter hatred is that by adhering to the teachings of Christ, the Church stands in opposition to the ways and the spirit of the world. Our Lord, knowing full well the opposition that His disciples would encounter, refers to this a second time in what is called His "High Priestly Prayer" (cf. John 17). In it, He prays to His Heavenly Father:

> I have given them Your word and the world has hated them for they do not belong to the world any more than I belong to the world. I do not ask You to take them out of the world, but to guard them from the Evil One. They are not of the world, just as I am not of the world. (John 17:14-16)

Jesus knows, as He is ready to leave the Apostles by His death and resurrection, that they will be left behind in the world. There they will experience its hatred, persecution, and opposition. So He prays to His Heavenly Father for them, not that they should come with Him, for He said, "I do not ask You to take them out of the world." Rather, He prays that the Father will protect them, "guard them from the Evil One." Jesus knows that the devil will stir up the spirit of the world against His disciples, against His Church. Therefore, Jesus prays that the Church will remain firm so that against Her, the very gates of Hell shall not prevail.[2]

Interestingly, a document of the first century entitled *Letter to Diognetus*, written by an anonymous sacred writer, vividly describes the bitter hatred of the world that had already arisen in that first Christian century:

---

2   It is clear that the world's opposition was foretold by Christ from the very beginning. Those who were willing to follow Him, therefore, should not have been under any illusions that the way would be easy.

Christians love all men but all men persecute them. Condemned because they are not understood, they are put to death but raised to life again. They live in poverty, but enrich many. They are totally destitute, but possess an abundance of everything. They suffer dishonor, but that is their glory. They are defamed, but vindicated. A blessing is their answer to abuse; deference their response to insult. For the good they do, they receive the punishment of malefactors, but even then they rejoice, as though receiving the Gift of Life. They are attacked by the Jews as aliens, they are persecuted by the Greeks, yet no one can explain the reason for this hatred. To speak in general terms, we may say that the Christian is to the world what the soul is to the body. As the soul is present in every part of the body, while remaining distinct from it, so Christians are found in all the cities of the world, but cannot be identified with the world. As the visible body contains the invisible soul, so Christians are seen as living in the world, but their religious life remains unseen. The body hates the soul and wars against it, not because of any injury the soul has done it, but because of the restriction the soul places on its pleasures. Similarly, the world hates Christians, not because they have done it any wrong, but because they are opposed to its enjoyments.

What was written in this letter to Diognetus in the first century could be echoed in each century since. The Church has suffered the opposition of the world in all its forms. Yet, the Church has never been overcome.[3]

---

3 There is one more point that should he noted from the *Letter to Diognetus*. The reason given in the letter as to why the world has always hated the Church is because the Church, by its moral teaching, passes judgement on the sinful ways of the world. In turn, the world hates the Church for this. We have a contemporary example of this opposition over the issue of right-to-life and abortion. We see the tremendous opposition to the Church by the pro-abortion forces. They despise the Catholic Church and her teaching because the Church condemns the world's claim to sexual license, and in turn teaches that sexuality is a gift of God and must be expressed only according to His moral laws. The pro-abortion forces obviously reject the Church's teaching that every new life conceived has a sacredness from God Himself that all must respect and never destroy.

At the same time, however, opposition to the Church has always drawn together the most unlikely of friends. We read in Psalm 2, a Psalm which refers to the coming Messiah:

> Why do the nations rage and the peoples utter folly? The kings of the earth rise up and the princes conspire together against the Lord and against His Anointed, "Let us break their fetters and cast their bonds from us." (Palms 2:1-3)

We see this conspiracy realized in the case of the condemnation of Our Lord. Herod, the Jewish king, and Pontius Pilate, the Roman governor, had been at odds with each other, vying for power and influence. However, they found a common enemy in Christ. In their opposition to Our Lord, they set aside their previous differences and forged a new friendship. We read in the Gospel of St. Luke:

> Herod and Pilate, who had previously been set against each other, became friends that day. (Luke 23:12)

Opposing the Falsehood of the World

How does the Church oppose the falsehood of the world? Jesus indicated in His Last Supper discourse that the Church would do this in three ways.

The Spirit of Truth Will Convict the World of Falsehood

First, Jesus foretold that the falsehood of the world will be opposed and ultimately overcome with the coming of the Holy Spirit. The Paraclete will come to convict the world as Jesus told the disciples:

> Yet I tell you the sober truth: It is for your good that I should go away. If I fail to go, the Advocate will never come to you; but if I depart, I will send Him to you. When He comes, He will expose sin and justice and condemnation to the world for what it is. Sin—because they refuse to believe in Me; then justice—because I am returning to the Father and you will see Me no more; and condemnation—because the Prince of this world has been condemned. (John 16:7-11)

Our Lord is saying here that a major part of the role of the Spirit of Truth is to oppose the falsehood and distortions of the world. Our Lord says that the Advocate will do this by proving the world wrong about three things: sin, justice, and condemnation. Let us look at each of these closely to understand what Our Lord means.

The Spirit Will Prove the World Wrong About "Sin"

In the Gospel of St. John, the great sin that is emphasized is the deliberate refusal by many of the people to believe that Jesus was Who He claimed to be, namely, the Messiah and the Son of God. Despite all His proofs, His miracles, His deeds of mercy and compassion, as well as His sublime teaching. Many of the people, especially their leaders, had hardened their hearts against Him. It was this sin of their unwillingness to believe that ultimately led them to reject Jesus. When the Holy Spirit would come, however, He would make many come to realize the wrong—the "sin"—they had committed when they had previously opposed Jesus and refused to accept Him. He would eventually convert their minds and hearts to recognize and accept Jesus as Son of God and Savior. He would also make them realize the "sin" of those who still refused to accept Jesus, of those whose hearts remained deliberately closed to Jesus despite all the evidence to the contrary.

The Spirit Will Prove the World Wrong About "Justice"

Many of Jesus' contemporaries had rejected His claim to be the Son of the Eternal Father. When they condemned Him as being guilty of blasphemy for daring to proclaim Himself to be God's Son, He died in disgrace and humiliation on the cross of Calvary. The people took His death in such disgrace and humiliation as a vindication of their rejection of Jesus. After all, they reasoned, if this were really God's Son, would

His Heavenly Father ever allow Him to die in such shame and suffering?

Yet, in reality, "justice" has now been done because the Father has raised up Jesus, His Son, from the dead by His glorious Resurrection. Jesus has triumphed still further by ascending to His place of glory in Heaven at the right hand of His Heavenly Father. With the assistance of the Spirit of Truth, the Apostles would preach this message boldly to the very ends of the earth. Furthermore, they would confirm this message with the many miraculous "signs and wonders" they would also work through the Spirit's power. This message and these miracles would condemn any who say that Jesus had not come from the Father, or that the Father did not support His Son and approve of His sacrificial death upon the cross. At the same time, this message would affirm those who accepted Jesus. It would strengthen their faith in the victory that Jesus had won by His triumphant Resurrection and glorious Ascension into Heaven.

The Spirit Will Prove the World Wrong About "Condemnation"

It was the devil himself who stirred the enemies of Jesus into rage and provoked them to seek His death upon the cross. Ironically, however, in God's plan, it was to be that very act of Jesus' death by which the devil himself would be defeated and his kingdom ultimately be destroyed. By Jesus' death, the judgment of condemnation has now been passed upon the devil who is referred to in Scripture as the "Prince of this world." Now his "kingdom" has been overcome. The Spirit of Truth bears witness to this condemnation of the "kingdom" of Satan by the establishment of the kingdom of Jesus in the Church. By His trial, passion, and ignominious death upon the cross, it was not really Jesus Who was condemned, but the devil who was condemned, because by His sacrificial death, Jesus saved us from our sins and from the power of Satan's kingdom. The Kingdom of Light has passed the judgment of condemnation on the Kingdom of Darkness!

The Spirit and the Apostles Jointly Give Witness to Jesus

The second way Jesus foretold that the Church would overcome the falsehood and opposition of the world would be through the Spirit of Truth and the Apostles jointly witnessing to Him. At the Last Supper Jesus spoke to the Apostles:

> When the Advocate comes, Whom I will send to you from the Father—the Spirit of Truth Who comes forth from the Father—He will bear witness on My behalf. But you, too, must bear witness as well, because you have been with Me from the beginning. (John 15:26-27)

Jesus is saying in this passage, as we just saw briefly above, that both the Apostles and the Spirit of Truth would witness to Him. The Apostles, of course, would do this by their preaching, their Christ-like example and, ultimately, by their deaths as martyrs. According to long-standing tradition, all the Apostles died as martyrs, except for St. John the Beloved, who died in exile. (The word "martyr" is taken from the Greek language and means a "witness".) The early Church saw the act of dying for Jesus, the act of martyrdom, as the ultimate witness to Him. The Apostles would give that heroic witness!

The Holy Spirit would also be witnessing to Jesus. He would do this, first of all, inwardly by strengthening the faith of the Apostles and all the other disciples of Jesus who had come to believe in Him. This strengthening would give them the conviction and courage needed to face the world's opposition.

The Advocate would also witness to Jesus outwardly by confirming the Apostles' preaching by the many miraculous "signs and wonders" He would work at their hands. He would accomplish great things to prove that the Apostles' message was true, namely, that Jesus had already won the victory for us. These powerful "signs and wonders" were manifestations of Jesus' victory!

The Apostles Will Be Consecrated in the Truth

Finally, Jesus foretold a third means by which the Church would overcome the falsehood and opposition of the world. He said it would be overcome because the Apostles will be consecrated by the "truth." In part of His *High Priestly Prayer*, Jesus prayed especially for the Apostles at the Last Supper:

> Father, consecrate them by means of truth—Your word is truth. As You have sent Me into the world, I have sent them into the world. I consecrate Myself for their sakes now, that they may be consecrated in truth (John 17:17-19)

Jesus prays that the Apostles will be "consecrated in truth." This means that they will be set apart or strengthened by means of truth. Our Lord further says in this prayer: "I consecrate Myself for their sakes now." Jesus, too, is willing to be consecrated in the "truth." This refers to His readiness to endure suffering and death upon the Cross. He is ready to lay down His life for His Apostles and, in fact, for the salvation of the whole world. This will be the ultimate sign of the "truth" that He had come from the Father, namely, His readiness to accept the Father's Will, no matter what suffering or sacrifice it would entail.

Jesus was willing to endure this for the sake of the Apostles, that they might also be consecrated in truth. This is why He wanted them to be consecrated (set apart) by this same "truth" or attitude He Himself had, and to be strengthened by living this "truth" in their daily lives, especially in their trials and sacrifices. In this way, they would possess and live by the same truth He possessed and by which He lived. They would be "consecrated" by the same truth by which Jesus was consecrated. It would be the work of the Spirit of Truth to bring about this consecration in the truth for each of the Apostles. Our Lord had told them that when the Spirit of Truth came, He would lead them into all truth; in fact, the Holy Spirit would take from Jesus' own truth and share this truth with them:

> When He comes, however, being the Spirit of Truth He will lead you to the whole truth. He will not speak on His own, but instead will speak only what He hears, and He will proclaim to you the things to come. In doing this, He will give glory to

Me, because He will have received from Me what He will proclaim to you. (John 16:13-14)

Falsehood from inside the Church

Up to this point we have looked at falsehood coming from outside the Church. Now let us look at a falsehood that is even more dangerous because it is often more subtle. This second kind of falsehood that the Spirit of Truth opposes is falsehood from within the Church. It can be even more devastating than the opposition of the world. We expect the opposition of the world; we do not expect the opposition and even unfaithfulness of one of our own members within the Church community. For example, it was one thing for the pagan governor Pilate, despite the famed Roman sense of justice, to condemn Jesus to death to please the crowd. It was also not very surprising that the Jewish high priest Caiaphas, a man of religious ambition and power, did the same out of pride and jealousy. But it was quite another thing for the Apostle Judas to hand Jesus, his Lord and Master, over to His enemies.[4]

---

4   I wonder how many times the words of Psalm 55 must have gone through the mind of Our Lord as His impending betrayal came near:

> If an enemy had reviled Me, I could have borne it; if he who hates Me had vaunted himself against Me, I might have hidden from him. But you, my other self, My companion and My bosom friend! You, whose comradeship I enjoyed; at whose side I walked in procession in the House of God! (Psalms 55:13-14)

Today we must admit sadly that much of the falsehood and confusion among our Catholic people comes from within the Church herself. Opinion is frequently offered in place of Sacred Tradition; expediency has often replaced sound doctrine; personal interpretation and popularity are often the norms used to determine what a person will believe rather than the official teachings of the Church's magisterium. Much of the negative attitude of the "world" has filtered into the Church, thereby making her responsibility to proclaim Christ's truth to the ends of the earth more difficult. Like a proverbial "fifth column" in war, this worldly attitude poses the threat of disrupting the Church from within.

Paul's Warning to Avoid Doctrinal Instability

St. Paul, in his Letter to the Ephesians, teaches us a powerful defense against this danger of falsehood from within. He warns his readers not to become doctrinally unstable, not to chase after every whimsical "new idea" in theological circles. His important message focuses on the need "to profess the truth in love":

> Let us, then, be children no longer, tossed here and there, carried about by every wind of doctrine that originates in human trickery and skill in proposing error. Rather, let us profess the truth in love and grow to the full maturity of Christ the Head. (Ephesians 4:14-15)

Certain people seem to possess a need to be theologically "trendy." These people read the latest books, or attend the lectures of the most "current" theologians, never critically evaluating what they read or hear. It seems to me that in the years since Vatican Council II, some people have been on a theological "roller coaster ride." They have gone from one theological approach to another (for example: radical theology, process theology, liberation theology, feminist theology), basically because it happens to be the "latest fad" in theological circles. The result is a theological "maze." There is little wonder that such persons become "confused" as to what they believe anymore as Catholics.

THE SPIRIT OF TRUTH CLARIFIES OUR CATHOLIC IDENTITY

We must always keep in mind that in accepting any teaching in theology, it must measure up to the norm of truth, as found in the sources of Revelation, namely, in Sacred Scripture and in Sacred Tradition as taught by the official Magisterium of the Church, the pope and the bishops in union with him. The Spirit of Truth helps us to evaluate and accept what is good and useful and solid in current teaching, while at the same time to reject whatever is contrary or detrimental to the Catholic Faith. To accept an "opinion" of a popular theologian just because the theologian is "current" is foolish and risks later regret. We cannot come to that full maturity St. Paul talks about if we are in error or confusion. Spiritual maturity implies a sufficiently clear and stable sense of identity regarding both who we are and who we are not. Error and confusion distort that clarity of identity and, thus, hinder our spiritual growth.

It is the role of the Spirit of Truth to form that clarity of identity both in the Universal Church as well as in each individual Catholic by assisting us to oppose every falsehood. He safeguards the official teachers within the Church community with His gift of infallibility, so that when they teach officially, their teachings are preserved free from all error. When the Catholic faithful in turn accept this teaching with the assent of faith, they become grounded upon the truth. With this truth as a contrasting light, they are enabled to recognize the darkness of falsehood for what it is, and then to oppose it by the powerful light of the Advocate, the Spirit of Truth!

REFLECTION QUESTIONS

1. What is your attitude towards all the "Catholic bashing" in the media happening in the world today?

2. Are you careful to evaluate the spiritual books you are reading, the spiritual tracts you are listening to, the religious instruction videos you are watching, or the bible studies that you want to get involved in, to ensure that they are faithful to the Magisterium of the Catholic Church?

3. Have you ever suffered as a result of defending a truth of the Catholic Faith? (e.g., not attending a same-sex wedding ceremony of a friend and losing that close friendship as a result, being jeered at by others while participating in a pro-life march or protest, etc.)

*Spirit of knowledge and piety, have
mercy on us.
Spirit of the fear of the Lord, have mercy
on us.
Spirit of grace and prayer, have mercy
on us.
Spirit of peace and meekness, have mercy
on us.
Spirit of modesty and innocence, have
mercy on us.
Holy Spirit, the Comforter, have mercy
on us.*

—LITANY OF THE HOLY SPIRIT

CHAPTER 8

THE ADVOCATE HELPS US TO DISCERN THE TRUTH

No matter how much we may study, it is not possible to come to know God unless we live according to His commandments, for God is not known by science, but by the Holy Spirit.

—St. Silouan the Athonite

IN THE LAST THREE CHAPTERS, we have looked at the Advocate as a divine "Defense Lawyer," countering ignorance, error, and falsehood. Now let us begin to look at the positive role of the Advocate as a divine "Prosecuting Attorney," promoting the truth of Christ and the Church in our lives.

The first role of the Advocate in fostering the truth is to help us to discern the truth. Truth and falsehood are not always easy to distinguish. Our Lord emphasizes this point in His parable of the wheat and the weeds. Until both the wheat and the weeds mature, a person cannot easily tell one from the other (cf. Matthew 13:24-30). It would take a skillful and experienced farmer to tell the difference before the wheat and the weeds mature. In a similar manner, evil often takes on the appearance of good. Only with the enlightenment of the Holy Spirit can we properly distinguish one from the other, especially in their earlier stages of growth.

THE "SENSE OF THE FAITHFUL"

To assist us in discerning truth from falsehood, the Holy Spirit gives us what is called "the sense of the faithful." We must distinguish this "sense of the faithful"[1] from the prerogative of "infallibility" enjoyed by certain members of the Church. Though they are related in a certain way, they are still distinct workings of the Holy Spirit.

Infallibility

The pope and the bishops in union with him constitute the official "magisterium" or "teaching authority" of the Church. They enjoy the special gift of "infallibility" when they teach the faithful in an official way. This means that they are guaranteed to be protected from doctrinal error in matters of faith and morals, whenever they teach in such a way that they intend to bind the consciences of all the faithful to accept and believe the particular truth or truths being taught. This gift of infallibility attaches to the official public teaching office in

---

1   In Latin, this is rendered either as *sensus fidei* (literally, the "sense of faith") or as *sensus fidelium* (literally, "the sense of the faithful").

the Church community which the pope and the bishops in union with him occupy.[2]

The Sense of the Faithful

The "sense of the faithful," on the other hand, resides with all the baptized, clergy, and laity alike, and not just the hierarchy. At the same time, while "infallibility" safeguards the "teaching" function of the official teachers of the Church, the "sense of the faithful" affects the act of "believing" on the part of all

---

2 Vatican Council II clearly reaffirmed the Catholic belief in infallibility which it says Christ gave to "His Church in defining doctrine pertaining to faith and morals." (cf. *Lumen Gentium,* ch. III, par. 25-26, p. 380)

Regarding the pope's infallibility, the Council states:

"The Roman Pontiff, head of the college of bishops, enjoys this infallibility in virtue of his office, when, as supreme pastor and teacher of all the faithful—who confirms his brethren in the faith—he proclaims in an absolute decision a doctrine pertaining to faith or morals."

Regarding the bishops, the Vatican Council teaches:

"Although the bishops, taken individually, do not enjoy the privilege of infallibility, they do, however, proclaim infallibly the doctrine of Christ on the following conditions: namely, when even though dispersed throughout the world but preserving for all that among themselves and with Peter's successor the bond of communion, in their authoritative teaching concerning matters of faith and morals, they are in agreement that a particular teaching is to be held definitively and absolutely. This is still more clearly the case when, assembled in an ecumenical council, they are, for the universal Church, teachers of and judges in matters of faith and morals, whose decision must be adhered to with the loyal and obedient assent of faith."

THE ADVOCATE

members of the Church. All the baptized, whether clergy or laity, must believe. They must make an act of faith or render the "obedience (or assent) of faith" to whatever truths the Church authentically teaches and proposes for belief. The "sense of the faithful" protects the baptized from believing something the Church does not teach (which may even in fact be contrary to her teaching), and it safeguards the belief in those truths the Church officially teaches, even if some of her members may actually be trying to reject or deny them. The Holy Spirit, by this "sense of the faithful," helps the faithful in general to hold on to all authentic truth and to resist denying or distorting or rejecting it in any way. The *Catechism of the Catholic Church* describes the "sense of the faithful" in the following way:

> All the faithful share in understanding and hand-
> ing on revealed truth. They have received the
> anointing of the Holy Spirit, Who instructs them
> (cf. 1 John 2:20, 27) and guides them into all
> truth (cf. John 16:13).

> The whole body of the faithful . . . cannot err in
> matters of belief. This characteristic is shown
> in the supernatural appreciation of faith (*sensus
> fidei*) on the part of the whole people, when "from
> the bishops to the last of the faithful," they man-
> ifest a universal consent in matters of faith and
> morals (*LG* 12; St. Augustine, *De praed. sanct.* 14,
> 27; PL 44, 980).

> By this appreciation of the faith, aroused and sus-
> tained by the Spirit of Truth, the People of God,

> guided by the sacred teaching authority (Mag-
> isterium), . . . receives . . . the faith, once for all
> delivered to the saints . . . The People unfailingly
> adhere to this faith, penetrate it more deeply with
> right judgment, and apply it more fully in daily
> life (*LG* 12; cf. Jude 3). (#91-93, p. 28)

The working of this "sense of the faithful" has been expressed in many ways, some of them almost humorous. For example, the Redemptorist, St. Clement Mary Hoff-bauer, used to say: "I have a Catholic nose. I can smell when something isn't just right." When I studied theology in the seminary years ago, we would occasionally come across questionable or "shaky" opinions by certain theological authors. These theological opinions were not exactly all they should have been, but neither were they clearly heretical. Such shaky opinions were usually labeled as "offensive to pious ears." This was a clever way of saying that their content was disturbing and usually left something to be desired in terms of orthodoxy.

THE EFFECTS OF THE SENSE OF THE FAITHFUL

We can summarize the effects of the "sense of the faithful" if we paraphrase (and alter to some degree) a famous saying of the great American President, Abraham Lincoln. He said:

> You can fool some of the people all of the time,
> and all of the people some of the time, but you
> can't fool all of the people all of the time.

Let us, for our purposes here, substitute the idea of being "in error" for the idea of being "fooled." We can then paraphrase his statement in regard to the "sense of the faithful," by stating:

> Some of the faithful can be in error some of the time, and some of the faithful can be in error all of the time, but all of the faithful cannot be in error at the same time.

"Some in Error Some of the Time"

Let us look at each statement. "Some of the faithful can be in error some of the time." This is obvious since even sincere members of the Church can be and have been in error or mistaken in regard to various doctrinal truths. Examples abound in Church history. Eminent theologians have been in error. Even saintly men and women declared as "Doctors of the Church" have been in error.[3] Bishops have been in error when they believed (and even taught) erroneous teachings apart from what the pope was teaching.[4] Now, if those in positions of teaching authority can be in error some of the time, it follows that some of the faithful will be in error through ignorance or wrong teaching at least some of the time.

---

3 For example, St. Thomas Aquinas, the great Angelic Doctor of the Church, did not believe in the Immaculate Conception of the Blessed Virgin Mary. Of course, at his time, this teaching was not yet a defined dogma of the Church.

4 It was said at the time of the Arian heresy, which denied the divinity of Jesus, that more bishops were Arian in their belief than were Catholic. This prompted St. Jerome to remark that "the Church awoke one day and found itself Arian."

"Some in Error All of the Time"

Let us now look at the second phrase: "Some of the faithful can be in error all of the time." This can happen when, through factors like intellectual pride or gravely immoral living, some of the faithful turn their backs upon the truth and live "outside the truth." It may be only a matter of time before such persons actually break away from their external unity with the believing Church community. The example of Judas Iscariot illustrates this point. When Our Lord preached about the Eucharist, promising to give His very flesh and blood to be our spiritual food and drink, He lost the crowds:

> Many of His disciples who were listening said: "This sort of talk is hard to endure! How can anyone take it seriously?" Jesus was fully aware that His disciples were complaining about what He had said. "Does this shake your faith?" He asked them . . . From this time on, many of His disciples broke away and would not remain in His company any longer. (John 6:60-61, 66)

But it seems He also lost Judas, too! When Our Lord asked His apostles if they would walk away with the crowd, St. Peter spoke the faith of the believing Church:

> Jesus then said to the Twelve, "Do you want to leave Me, too?" Simon Peter answered Him. "Lord, to whom would we go? You have the words of eternal life. We have come to believe and are convinced that You are God's Holy One" (John 6:67-69)

Then Our Lord remarked in reference to Judas.

> "Did I Myself not choose the Twelve of you? Yet
> one of you is a devil." Now He was speaking about
> Judas, son of Simon Iscariot, because he, though
> one of the Twelve, was going to hand Jesus over.
> (John 6:70-71)

When Our Lord said to His Apostles that if they did not believe His teaching about the Eucharist they should go away with the crowd that was leaving Him (who also did not believe), Judas should have left, but he did not. Yet it appears clear enough that Judas did not believe—he had the "devil of disbelief." But he did not honestly walk away either. This was the beginning of a major problem! Despite physically staying, Judas' heart was separated from Jesus. As time went on, he became further and further removed from Jesus until he ended up betraying his beloved Lord and Master. From the moment he did not believe, Judas was in error "all of the time."

"All Cannot be in Error at the Same Time"

Finally, we have the statement that "all of the faithful cannot be in error at the same time." Here the Holy Spirit, through His grace of the "sense of the faithful," would never permit the whole Church, all of the faithful, clergy and laity, to be in error at the same time regarding a certain point, whether permanently or even for a limited time. Truth must be present, believed and lived, at every moment somewhere in the Church. The Holy Spirit safeguards the Church's possession of the truth. Let us go back to the earlier example of the heresy of Arianism. We mentioned that many bishops at that time actually believed in Arianism. They probably constituted a majority of the bishops of the day. But what is very important to recall, to illustrate our point here, is the fact that not all the bishops believed the Asian heresy and not all denied Jesus' divinity. A number taught the true doctrine about Jesus' divinity. Furthermore, the bishop of Rome, the pope, believed in Jesus' divinity and opposed Arianism. This is an illustration of the point we were making: "all of the faithful cannot be in error at the same time." The Holy Spirit, the Spirit of Truth, sees to it that many of the clergy and laity always remain loyal to the truths God has revealed and the Church teaches, even in the most difficult times in Church history.

ALL PARTS OF TRUTH MUST FIT TOGETHER

The basic reason for this "sense of the faithful" is that truth has a quality called "congruence." This means that all of its parts must harmonize or fit together. Truth must form a totally integrated unity, like all the pieces of a completed jigsaw puzzle fitting together. If something is "not true," it will not, indeed, it cannot, "fit in" with what is "true." What the Holy Spirit gives us is a sense of knowing when something "just does not fit in." For example, the Church has always traditionally taught that sexual relations are morally right only between a husband and wife in the sacrament of Marriage. If someone teaches that sexual relations "between two consenting adults who really love each other" is morally acceptable even outside of marriage, we have a teaching that does not "fit in."

One outstanding modern theologian, Fr. Hans Urs von Balthasar, expresses this idea in another way. He says that truth is "symphonic." Like a great symphony, all the melodies must blend together. Any strident or discordant notes will threaten to destroy the symphony's harmony and beauty. So, too, falsehood threatens to destroy the harmony as well as the beauty of truth.

The "congruence" quality of truth (that all its parts must fit together properly) is essential. A watch will not run if even one essential part is broken or missing or out of place because the other parts need to synchronize with that particular part. The same principle holds true for our spiritual growth. If we want to be on the correct pathway leading to the Lord and grow properly in our spiritual life, we need to possess His truth. Discerning the truth from falsehood (and even from error and ignorance, as we have seen earlier) is essential to coming to possess that truth. This requires that we accept the truth by faith and hold to it firmly and faithfully, while rejecting that which is false.

Faith and Discerning the Truth

Faith Is Not "Contrary to Reason"

There are some important points we should keep in mind with respect to discerning the truth. The first is that some of the deep mysteries of our Catholic Faith are beyond the capacity of our limited minds to grasp or understand completely. Such religious mysteries are "beyond reason." But they are not "contrary to reason." In other words, they are not a contradiction. Authentic truth does not contradict our reasoning ability, though at times it may go beyond our mind's ability to understand it fully or to explain it to others. The discerning light of the Holy Spirit assists our gift of faith to help us recognize when there is a contradiction in a certain teaching (which we then would not accept) as opposed to an evident mystery which we do accept (even though we cannot fully explain it) because God revealed it and the Church officially teaches it.

Faith Cannot Always Explain "How"

This brings us to a second important point to remember about faith and discerning the truth. It is simply the fact that we must distinguish between what we call the "content" (or the "what") of a religious mystery and the "explanation" (or the "how") of that same mystery. The "content" refers to the general meaning of the mystery, whereas the "explanation" refers to the ability to explain how this mystery is so. Faith enables us to accept the "content" or the "what" of our religious truths. However, faith, especially with regard to the deeper truths and teachings of the Catholic Church, does not necessarily mean we can explain fully the "how" of these mysteries.

In the Church, it is the role of theologians to offer various explanations of "how" these mysteries can be so; but in most cases. such explanations are necessarily quite limited. It is important to remember that our faith or belief in these revealed truths requires that we have an adequate understanding of "what" these truths mean, even if we may not be able to explain fully "how" they can be so or "how" they will be accomplished by God in the future. Remember, also, that our faith in these truths does not rest on theologians' explanations of them, but on the fact that Jesus revealed them and the Catholic Church teaches them.

Faith Still Accepts What Reason Cannot Understand

A third point should be evident from what has just been said. If a mystery of the Catholic Faith cannot be fully explained, it does not mean that mystery is not true, not real. It just means it is too deep for most people to grasp easily. Let us use an example. Most people cannot scientifically explain the process of splitting an atom, but that does not mean that such a process does not exist. It only means that the ability of most people to explain it is too limited. Now, if someone were to conclude that because most people cannot explain the process of splitting the atom, then such a process does not really exist, that would contradict the facts, since such a process does indeed exist.

If we apply this point to the Catholic teaching on the Holy Eucharist, I believe many people, because they cannot explain it, dismiss the Catholic belief as unimportant or they look upon the Holy Eucharist as just a "symbol" of Jesus' Body. In this way, they do not have to deal with trying to explain how what still looks, feels, smells, and tastes like bread is now the Body, Blood, Soul, and Divinity of Jesus Christ, the Son of God and the Savior of the world. Yet, it is clear from Scripture that, as He took bread, blessed it, broke it, and gave it to the Apostles, Jesus said, "Take this;

this is My Body" (cf. Mark 14:22). This is what the Catholic Church from the very beginning, 2000 years ago, has always understood, believed, taught, and practiced. Any difficulty to explain a revealed mystery fully in human terms does not simply make that mystery go away!

THE SPIRIT OF TRUTH
HELPS US DISCERN TRUTH

We seem to need the Holy Spirit's help in discerning the truth more today than ever. We must be able to sift through the overwhelming maze of religious opinions and statements that come to us from all sides in today's world, some from where we expect it and others from where we do not.

It is essential to keep in mind, as mentioned earlier, that today many writings by so-called "Catholic" authors really stray far from authentic Church teaching. Seeming to lack a certain critical concern and care for truth, their writings contain much that we can only label as ignorant, erroneous or false. As a result, these writings have led to a great deal of confusion and spiritual harm in the Church today.

One example that immediately stands out relates to the issue of abortion. In her official teaching, the Catholic Church has always condemned abortion as the direct killing of an innocent unborn child created by God. She has taught consistently that it is a mortal sin for any Catholic to obtain an abortion knowingly, or for any medical person or other individual to help that person procure the abortion. Despite such a clear and unquestionable moral teaching, we still have groups who call themselves "Catholics for Abortion" or

"Pro-Choice Catholics." Such titles are complete contradictions. "Catholic" and "Pro-Abortion" are totally opposed. In the thought of Pope St. John Paul II, they represent "The Culture of Life" and "The Culture of Death," respectively. To try to reconcile them, or to identify one with the other, would be a real contradiction. A Catholic simply cannot be both at the same time, because each mutually excludes the other. Some Catholics say—because of a prevailing confusion among so many in the Church today—that they actually think they can be both. But such thinking would certainly be a gross distortion of the truth so prevalent in our secularized society.

These are difficult times for loyalty in the Church. Truth is not accorded much importance or respect in today's society. It has been replaced with principles of "expedience" like: "whatever works," "whatever feels good," "whatever people want to hear"! We might well believe St. Paul was actually describing our own present situation when he wrote to his disciple Timothy:

> The time will come when people will not tolerate
> sound teaching, but, following their own desires,
> will surround themselves with teachers who tickle
> their ears. They will stop listening to the truth and
> will turn to fables. (2 Timothy 4:3-4)

The Spirit's gift of discernment, however, can produce amazing effects in all of us, even in those who have had limited opportunity for theological studies. A story is told about a Franciscan brother-friar in England around the turn of the century. He was attending a talk by a popular theologian. About half way through the talk, the brother stood up and began to walk out of the auditorium. One of the other friars with him whispered: "Brother, sit down. It's embarrassing for you to walk out during this theologian's talk." The brother answered. "But what he's saying is heresy." The other friar responded: "It can't be. He is one of the most outstanding speakers in England." The brother responded again: "I don't care if he's outstanding; what he's saying is heresy." The brother walked out. Some time later the theologian also walked out—right out of the Catholic Church! The brother had heard something in the talk that did not "fit in" with the teaching of the Church. He heard something that was "offensive to pious ears," even though others could not hear it yet. The Spirit of Truth was no doubt at work, helping that friar to discern truth from falsehood. We, too, need this same Spirit of Truth to guide us all through the growing sense of confusion that has upset so many in the Church today.

Having said all this, a word of caution may be in order here. We certainly do not want to encourage people to see a heretic in every pulpit or to judge every misstatement they hear as an indication that the preacher is disloyal to the magisterium of the Church. We must be vigilant without becoming vigilantes; quick to hear, slow to judge, always loving those who may disagree with us, following the example of Our Lord Himself.

A "CATHOLIC SENSE"

St. Paul tells us that we must have "the mind of Christ" (cf. 1 Corinthians 2:16) and that our "attitude must be that of Christ" (cf. Philippians 2:5). He means that as we grow in our spiritual lives, we must become more like Christ in our outlook and actions. We must think with His thoughts, judge by His standards, and live by His commandments. In short, we gradually become changed into His likeness. But as we are putting on the mind of Christ, we also end up putting on the mind of the Church. We acquire what is called a "Catholic sense."[5] This is a special effect of the Holy Spirit, making us love and cherish our Catholic Faith. It is like a sense of family, bonded together by a common call of our Heavenly Father and by Jesus' love, concerned and caring for one another. It penetrates our minds and hearts, so that we come to view life in the light of the Catholic Church's teachings and uphold her moral values in our daily lives. It makes us ready to renounce our own personal views in order to "think with the Church,"[6] always and in all things! It fills us with a special reverence and honor for what the Church holds as sacred, especially her sacraments and saints. It fills us with a filial piety of love and honor for all her members, "those of the household of the Faith" (cf. Galatians 6:10), but especially her leaders, the pope and the bishops and the priests. It moves us to promote the works and welfare of the Church, and come to her aid in times of need or persecution.

This "Catholic sense" follows from the close link between Jesus and His Church. St. Augustine expressed it in the

---

5 A "Catholic sense" (in Latin, *sensus Catholicus*) is very similar to "the sense of the faithful." Another similar expression is the "sense of the Church" (in Latin, *sensus Ecclesiae*).

6 The Latin phrase, *sentire cum Ecclesia*, is translated "to think (or feel) with the Church."

beautiful terms of married love, comparing Jesus to the Bridegroom and the Church to His Bride. He said that if anyone loves the Bridegroom (Jesus) they must also love His Bride (the Church). On the other hand, to disregard or disdain the Bride (the Church) is to neglect or reject the Bridegroom (Jesus).

The Example of St. Francis

St. Francis was someone who possessed this "Catholic sense" in an outstanding way. His life was marked by a deep love and constant loyalty to the Church. In fact, his call to personal holiness and his ministry to God's people are linked inseparably with the Church. An ancient antiphon or phrase used in the liturgical celebration of the Feast of St. Francis expresses this quality so clearly:

> Francis, a thoroughly Catholic and Apostolic man, taught that the faith of the Roman Church must be kept and that priests are to be revered above all other men.

St. Francis sought the direction of the Church in the person of the popes. For example, when he had his first eleven followers, he realized that God was using him to begin a new community of "penitents" in the Church. He addressed his eleven friars one day:

> I see, brothers, that God in His mercy means to increase our company: let us therefore go to our holy Mother the Roman Church and lay before the Supreme Pontiff what Our Lord has begun

to work through us; so that with his consent and direction we may continue what we have undertaken. (*Omnibus*, "Legend of the Three Companions", ch. XII, #46, p. 933)

St. Francis had no doubts that Jesus had called him personally to his vocation. But in his love for and allegiance to the Church, he wanted Pope Innocent III as the Vicar of Christ to send him and his eleven followers out to preach repentance, just as Jesus Himself had sent St. Peter and the other eleven Apostles out to preach the Gospel. In his love for and devotion to the Church, he wanted the special blessing of the Church. This attitude he had toward the Holy Father, St. Francis extended toward the bishops, especially Bishop Guido Secundi of Assisi, who befriended Francis from the very beginning of his conversion.

St. Francis, in order to assure that his Order would always remain loyal to the pope and to the Roman Catholic Church, incorporated his "Catholic sense" into his way of life. For example, in his earlier written Rule of 1221, he required faithfulness to the teachings of the Catholic Church for membership in his Order:

All the friars are bound to be Catholic and live and speak as such. Anyone who abandons the Catholic Faith or practice by word or deed must be absolutely excluded from the Order, unless he repents . . . (*Omnibus*, Rule of 1221, ch. 19, p. 46)

Later on, St. Francis put obedience and respect for the Holy Father both at the beginning and the end of his Rule of

1223. He wanted his Order to be "utterly subject and submissive to the Church. And so, firmly established in the Catholic Faith . . ." (*Omnibus*, Rule of 1223, ch. 12, p. 64)

No doubt the Holy Spirit inspired this great loyalty to the teaching and guidance of the Roman Catholic Church in the saint of Assisi and moved him to make it an essential element of his Order. St. Francis bequeathed his "Catholic sense" as a major part of the legacy he handed on to his friars and other followers for all time to come.

SONS AND DAUGHTERS OF THE CHURCH

When men or women live their Catholic Faith with love, joy, loyalty, and dedication, especially when it is characterized by this "Catholic sense," they truly deserve to be called "sons of the Church" and "daughters of the Church."[7] Some of the greatest saints spoke proudly of their filial devotion and relationship to Holy Mother Church. St. Teresa of Avila, at the moment of her death, described herself saying, "I am a daughter of the Church." She truly was—this woman who was a mystic, a spiritual writer, a reformer of religious life, an ardent lover of Jesus, and the first female "Doctor of the Church." St. Elizabeth Ann Seton told her religious, "Be daughters of the Church! Be daughters of the Church!" These religious Sisters were deeply in love with the Church. With their foundress, they are credited with

---

7   As St. Cyprian (d. 258 AD), bishop and martyr, said so many centuries ago: "He cannot have God for Father who does not have the Church for Mother!"

establishing the Catholic School system in America, educating over the years literally millions of young people in the basic understanding of their Catholic Faith.

In my room hangs a picture of Pope St. John Paul II embracing Venerable Archbishop Fulton J. Sheen in St. Patrick's Cathedral in New York City in the Fall of 1979. At the time, the Holy Father was greeting many members of the Church hierarchy in the sanctuary area of the cathedral. Archbishop Sheen was well up in age and had undergone heart surgery only a few years before. When Pope John Paul II saw the archbishop, he went over to him, embraced him, and paid him a sign of special respect, saying, "You have written and spoken well of Jesus Christ; you are a loyal son of the Church!" The Spirit of Truth had worked abundantly in Archbishop Fulton J. Sheen's life. The fruit of this was evident to all.

When I read that account. I thought to myself, "What more beautiful words could be used to describe a person's life than to call him or her a loyal 'son or daughter of the Church'!" May God grant that every Catholic man or woman would be worthy of such a title!

REFLECTION QUESTIONS

1. The "congruence" quality of truth is essential—all of its parts must fit together properly. Do you believe and live your Catholic faith in a congruent way?

2. Do you strive to have the mind and attitude of Christ and of the Church in all that you do?

3. Do you have a "Catholic sense"? In what ways do you cherish and express your love for your Catholic faith?

Holy Spirit, the Sanctifier, have mercy on us.
Holy Spirit, Who governs the Church, have mercy on us.
Gift of God, the Most High, have mercy on us.
Spirit Who fills the universe, have mercy on us.
Spirit of the adoption of the children of God, have mercy on us.

—LITANY OF THE HOLY SPIRIT

CHAPTER 9

THE ADVOCATE ENABLES
US TO LIVE IN THE TRUTH

*To lovers of the truth, nothing can be put before God and
hope in Him.*

—St. Basil

THE HOLY SPIRIT ALSO HELPS us to live the truth.
Much of the confusion in the Church today does not
begin in the mind but in the heart. Falsehood oftentimes does
not stem from what people want to think but from how they
want to live. For example, King Henry VIII brought about
the break of the Church in England from the unity of the
Roman Catholic Church essentially as a result of his desire
to get an annulment so that he could marry again (although
he was already properly married in the Church). Added to
this was his desire to get increased revenues for his royal trea-
sury (which he ultimately did get by suppressing religious
houses in England and seizing their wealth). He knew the

truth.[1] The tragedy he brought into the history of the Catholic Church in England was his failure to live the truth.

LIVING THE TRUTH MEANS MAKING A CHOICE

Living the truth means making the Gospel and the Church's teachings an essential part of our daily lives. This is important, first, for living out our Christian lives. Our Lord ends His most famous sermon, the Sermon on the Mount, with a striking comparison. Having just offered His listeners the heart of all His great moral teaching, He tells them they now have a choice to make. They must choose either to accept His teaching or to reject it, to live by it or to live by their own standards.

> Everyone who hears these words of Mine and puts them into practice is like the wise man who built his house on rock. When the rain fell and the floods came and the winds blew and beat against his house, it did not fall, because its foundations were firmly set on rock. Everyone who hears these words of Mine but does not put them into practice is like the foolish man who built his house on sand. The rain fell and the floods came and the winds blew and beat against his house.

---

1   Ironically, he had written a work defending the Catholic Faith against the earlier attacks of Martin Luther in Germany, for which work the Pope had given him the title, "Defender of the Faith."

And it collapsed under all this and was completely
ruined. (Matthew 7:24-27)

We, too, must make this choice: will we build on rock
or sand? To live the truth is to build on rock. Believing Our
Lord's teachings and living by His commandments will
serve as the solid foundation of our lives. When life's storms
come our way—and they do for everyone at some time or
other—they will not be able to tear us from the solid foundation of truth. A good conscience, a sense of peace, a faith that
moves mountains, a hope that is still encouraging us when
everything around us looks hopeless, a love that knows it
is loved in return—these are the fruits of truth that emerge
within us in life's difficult times.

In contrast, to reject the truth is to build on sand. The
sand of life is falsehood that produces restless anxiety, a
reproachful conscience, disbelief, and despair in the face of
life's trials and misfortunes. Such sand will never serve as a
solid foundation during life's storms.

LIVING THE TRUTH MEANS
CONQUERING OUR SINFUL PASSIONS

To live the truth requires that we strive by God's grace to
conquer and subdue our passions and sinful desires and
inclinations. This is vitally important. Our passions not
only can lead us into sin, but they can also block us from
seeing the truth clearly, or being open enough to accept it.
This occurs whenever our passions have a hold on us, when
we are attached to them and unwilling even to attempt to

restrain them. Habits of sin, to which we are attached, likewise prevent us from being decisive in changing our lives. As we conquer our passions, however, we come to see the truth more clearly. It is like scales falling from the eyes of our soul! Furthermore, as we break our attachments to sin and free ourselves from their addictive enslavement, we become freer inwardly to acknowledge what God wants of us. This is why Our Lord could say:

> If you live according to My teaching, you are truly My disciples; then you will know the truth, and the truth will set you free . . . I give you My assurance, everyone who lives in sin is the slave of sin . . . (John 8:31-32, 34)

We also begin to experience a sense of order coming into our soul, leading to greater peace, for as St. Augustine has said, "Peace is the tranquillity of order." St. Peter gives us an insight into what is happening when he writes:

> Since you have purified your souls through obedience to the truth for sincere brotherly love, you should love one another earnestly from the heart. (1 Peter 1:22)

Since our passions turn us inward and focus us on self-love, as we overcome them, we become free enough in our souls to turn outward toward others. We can now focus on the love of our neighbor. This is the fruit of our "obedience to God's truth," which simply means living by His teachings and His commandments.

"The Spirit and the Flesh are Directly Opposed . . ."

So the struggle to overcome our passions and sinful attachments is one of spiritual life and death. It finds us drawn on the one hand by the life and truth of the Holy Spirit and on the other hand by the cravings of the flesh that lead to sin and spiritual death. St. Paul tells us that the Spirit and the flesh do battle against each other because they are directly opposed to each other:

> My point is that you should live according to the Spirit and you will not yield to the cravings of the flesh. The desires of the flesh are opposed to the Spirit and the Spirit is opposed to the flesh. They are opposed to each other so that you may not always do what your will intends. (Galatians 5:16-17)

St. Paul tells us here that the condition necessary for growth in holiness is for us to overcome our sins and evil inclinations. These in turn are fed by our passions and sinful desires. Therefore, in order to make any progress in loving God and being faithful to His truth, we must uproot these sinful desires from our souls, as far as possible by God's grace. This—we know only too well from human experience—is a real struggle! We want to live as good Christians; we make good resolutions; we pray and ask God for the strength we need. Then a temptation comes our way and our resolve is broken, our good resolutions vanish, our passions triumph! We must get up and try again.

An old saying puts it well: "A saint is nothing more than a sinner who keeps trying!" This is why St. Paul says that we do not do what our wills resolve to do. He tells us of his own struggle between his "inner self," which was attracted to God and wanted to do His Will, and his "flesh," which was the prisoner of his sinful passions (cf. Romans 7:14-25). This is our common Christian experience in this life.

PUTTING OFF THE "OLD SELF" AND PUTTING ON THE "NEW SELF"

The Holy Spirit helps us in our weakness so that by living the truth we will conquer the disorder of our passions within us. St. Paul dealt with this issue more fully in his letter to the Church community at Ephesus. His converts there were formerly pagan Gentiles whose standards and behavior prior to their conversion had been quite immoral. St. Paul, as a watchful shepherd of his flock, became afraid that they might drift back into their old sinful ways. They seemed to be in danger of following after the example of their pagan neighbors who lacked the moral teaching of Christ to guide them in the true way of salvation. So he warned his converts:

> I say this and solemnly bear witness in the Lord—you must no longer live as the pagans do, with their futile reasoning. Their understanding is clouded and they are alienated from God's life because of their ignorance, which is caused by the hardening of their hearts. (Ephesians 4:17-18)

St. Paul's words here stress that it is the pagans' lack of knowing moral truth in their lives that was leading them to fall into sins of immorality: "futile reasoning . . . understanding clouded . . . ignorance . . . hardening of their hearts." What he is telling his converts at Ephesus is that, if they neglect the guidance of the Spirit of Truth, they will end up in this same sad situation. St. Paul then goes on to describe for his Ephesian converts the results of their pagan neighbors' lack of true moral understanding. He warned that the same thing could happen to them if they were not vigilant:

> They have grown callous and have given themselves over to lust, greedily pursuing every sort of lewd conduct. That is not how you learned Christ, not if you heard about him and were taught the truth as it is in Jesus. (Ephesians 4:19-21)

Here, St. Paul points out the sinful conduct, especially of a sexual nature, that had become the very lifestyle of the pagans. Then notice how he moves from "they" (pagans) to "you" (the Christians at Ephesus), reminding them that this must not be their lifestyle. "Learning Christ" means that now they must conquer the passions of the flesh before these passions conquer and imprison them once again.

One of the hardest aspects of trying to live the Christian life in society today is no doubt having to live among people who, perhaps through little or no fault of their own, never learned about God's commandments and moral standards. Their pursuit of pleasure and carefree living are a real snare to those who are trying to live sincere Christian lives because the latter experience their own weaknesses pulling at them from inside. St. Paul knew the importance of proper moral teaching if Christians are to be prepared to do battle against their sins and passions. We, too, need "the truth as it is in Jesus" in our own neo-pagan society of today as much as the earliest Christians at Ephesus needed it in the pagan society of their day. St. Paul spoke of the need for "conversion." He described "the truth as it is in Jesus":

> You must put aside your former way of life and the old self which is corrupted by deceitful desires and illusions, and acquire a fresh, spiritual way of thinking. You must put on that new self created in God's image, whose justice and holiness are born of truth. (Ephesians 4:22-24)

St. Paul is saying to the Ephesians (and to us also) that there are two "selves" possible to a person: the "old self" and the "new self." The "old self" refers to their lives when they were rooted in sin and self-centered pleasure and immoral living. This was what they were as pagans. This had its roots in two forces at work within them: their "deceitful desires" and their "illusions."

Dealing with Our Deceitful Desires and Illusions

These "deceitful desires" and "illusions" are the forces—results of Original Sin at work within each person—that corrupt the "old self," leading it to "deteriorate" morally. Our "deceitful desires" are the passions within us that blindly crave pleasure, power, wealth, and every other form of self-centeredness.

Our "illusions" are the "rationalizations" that we use to justify the satisfaction of our desires and passions. "Illusions"
are distortions of truth and of reality that make it possible
for us to cloud over our view of reality, color it any shade we
want, and then appease our consciences that certain moral
evils are not really wrong. This makes it possible for us to do
wrong and not feel guilty about it.

What are some of these rationalizations? A common one
is the idea: "Today, everybody is doing it!" (But each person
will be judged by God for what he or she does, not for what
everybody else does!) Another rationalization is: "The times
have changed!" (But God and the commandments have not!)
Another one is: "God understands." (Yes, He does; but still,
did He not command us to do certain things and not to do
other things in spite of His being "understanding"?)

Another form of illusion which is popular today is
"denial"[2], to deny the wrong we have done. Sometimes,
along with "denial," a person may add "projection"—blaming
others for his or her own wrongdoing. For example, if such
a person is accused of doing something wrong, he denies

---

2   One of the areas where denial is taking a heavy toll is in the area
of abortion. I once heard of a survey in which several women were
asked if they had had an abortion. One-half of those who had abortions answered "no"; that was denial because they had actually had
abortions. In such cases, terrible pangs of guilt in the conscience
are often repressed, sometimes for many years, until the person can
courageously face the truth and honestly admit any wrongdoing,
make their peace with God and themselves, and then let the guilt go.
At that point, the pain of the "denial" will end. This is another instance
where the words of Jesus prove so real: "The truth will set you free!"

any responsibility or guilt by projecting blame on others: "So-and-so made me do it!"

"Illusions" try to justify the wrong we do. Instead of changing our immoral conduct to conform to God's commandments, we attempt to change God's laws or commandments to conform to our immoral conduct. With our passions enticing us in our hearts and our illusions justifying us in our heads, our moral self deteriorates. Venerable Archbishop Fulton J. Sheen summed it up well: "If we don't live what we believe, we will end up believing what we live."

Acquiring a "Spiritual Way of Thinking"

St. Paul challenged the Ephesians to acquire "a fresh, spiritual way of thinking" in order to counteract the thinking of the "flesh." This is our "new self." This "spiritual way of thinking" will lead us to a "justice and holiness born of truth." It is important to note that "illusion" rests on a lie or distortion. If truth increases within us, it will eventually destroy any such illusions we have. Truth, like a powerful light, pierces through the darkness of our illusions and exposes them for the distortions they really are.

To acquire this "fresh, spiritual way of thinking," to put on this "new self" or this "new man" created in God's image (that is, in the likeness of Christ), St. Paul told his converts at Ephesus to start overcoming their sins by the practice of the opposite virtues. He told them that if they are lying, they must learn to speak the truth; if they are angry, they must learn to control their temper, especially so that their anger does not just carry over to the next day without any effort to deal with it; if they are stealing, they should get a job and earn an honest living; if they are speaking evil things that hurt their neighbor, they must learn to say good things that will help them (cf. Ephesians 4:25-29). He summed it up with a striking contrast between how the "old self" of the flesh had acted and how the "new self" in the Spirit must live:

> Get rid of all bitterness, all passion and anger, harsh words, slander, and malice of every kind. In place of these, be kind to one another, compassionate, and mutually forgiving, just as God has forgiven you in Christ. (Ephesians 4:31-32)

To practice these virtues we need the Holy Spirit. He will give us the truth we need to know them, the love we need to motivate us, and the courage we need to live them. St. Paul also says:

> Do nothing to sadden the Holy Spirit with Whom you were sealed against the day of redemption. (Ephesians 4:30)

Since the Holy Spirit is God, we cannot literally make Him "sad," because we really cannot do anything to affect God directly. He is infinitely beyond anything like that. However, we can bring remorse to our own consciences by sin, and this will hinder the work of the Holy Spirit in us. This will, indeed, be a true "sadness" within us, where the Holy Spirit dwells!

We Need to Live the Truth in Order to Share It Effectively with Others

It should be evident that we all need to live the truth, not only for our own personal salvation and eternal life, but also for our continued sanctification and growth in holiness in this life. However, another important reason to live the truth is so that we might be able to share it with others.

Living the Truth Brings Us "Purity of Heart"

When we live the truth, God's law guides us. As we strive to keep His commandments, we must necessarily struggle against our sinful tendencies and attachments. If we struggle consistently and ardently, we will overcome them and subdue them by God's grace. In this way, we become free of domination by our passions and manipulation by our illusions. The result of this elimination of sin and this strengthening of virtue is a growing "purity of heart." Jesus assures us in His teaching on the Beatitudes that "the pure of heart . . . shall see God." (cf. Matthew 5:8)

Here is how "purity of heart" affects us. Anyone who is preoccupied with material possessions, sensual pleasures, or narcissistic self-concern has little time or interest in spiritual things However, once the human spirit is set free from these things by a counter-focus on God, spiritual things become very attractive. After all, our minds were made for God's truth and our hearts for His love. St. Augustine put it so well when he wrote: "God, You have made our hearts for

Yourself, and they are ever restless until they rest in You!" Like heliotrope plants that naturally turn toward the sunlight, we are instinctively drawn to God the freer we become of any obstacles that keep us from reaching out to Him. As St. Elizabeth Ann Seton once said, "Who can hold back the soul that God sets free?"

"Purity of Heart" Clarifies and Intensifies the Truth

But an increasing "purity of heart" in the soul has still another great effect. It allows the Advocate, the Spirit of Truth, to work more intensely in our minds and hearts. His gifts work more effectively in us, especially: (1) Knowledge, which helps us know what we should believe, (2) Understanding, which helps us penetrate spiritual truths more deeply, and (3) Wisdom which helps us to relish spiritual things. The result is that we come to grasp the truths of our Catholic Faith with a marvelously clear insight, a depth of conviction, and a clarity of expression.

Example of St. Francis

St. Francis, because he had attained such a high degree of "purity of heart" by his freedom from the world and its empty attractions, achieved a remarkable insight into the truths of Sacred Scripture. St. Bonaventure, a Doctor of the Church, writes about this in one of his accounts of the life of St. Francis:

> St. Francis had never studied Sacred Scripture, but unwearied application to prayer and the continual practice of virtue had purified his spiritual

vision, so that his keen intellect was bathed in the radiance of eternal light and penetrated its depths. Free from every stain, his genius pierced to the heart of its mysteries and by affective love he entered where theologians with their science stand outside. Once he had read something in the sacred books and understood its meaning, he impressed it indelibly on his memory; anything he had once grasped carefully, he meditated upon continually. (St. Bonaventure, *Major Life of St. Francis*, in *Omnibus*, Franciscan Herald Press, Chicago, 1973, pp. 711-712)

This effect of his "purity of heart" reached even to his preaching of the truth to others. No one can preach or teach more effectively or with greater persuasion than someone who shares with others what he himself believes. The message takes on a certain "authority" from the very conviction of the person speaking. People can sense that he really believes what he is saying, and not merely giving "the party line." On the other hand, if someone does not live the message they share with others, it sounds hollow. The speaker's life does not back up his words. To put it simply: if a cook eats his own cooking, it's a good sign; if he doesn't, everybody eats at their own risk! An old principle in the study of Philosophy states: "No one can give what they do not have." St. Teresa of Calcutta put it even more simply: "No one can give what they do not live!" Living the truth by the grace of the Spirit of Truth is the best assurance for proclaiming the truth faithfully. Again, we see this in the example of St. Francis:

Francis was not an experienced teacher, but he had no lack of knowledge, so that he was able to resolve doubtful questions and bring all their implications to light. There is nothing strange in the fact that he should have been enlightened by God to understand the Scriptures: by his perfect conformity with Christ he practiced the truths which are contained in them and carried their Author in his heart by the abundant infusion of the Holy Spirit. (*Ibid.*, pp. 712-713)

THE POWER OF EXAMPLE

We cannot help others to accept something we ourselves do not accept! A story in the life of St. Francis helps to illustrate this point. One day, he and another friar were entering a town. He said to the friar: "Brother, we are going to preach in this town." So they walked into the town together. As they came to the town square. the other friar thought that both St. Francis and he were going to stop walking and start preaching to the people. But they did not; they just kept on walking without saying a word to anyone. As they were coming to the other end of the town and were about to leave it, the surprised friar turned to St. Francis and said, "Brother Francis, I thought we were going to preach in this town?" St. Francis replied, "We just did!"

Example often speaks louder than words! Good Christian example is a powerful means of sharing the truth of God, His reality, with others. After all, a holy Christian life makes God very real to others. Furthermore, we never know how our good example will affect others. Someone once wrote: "Your life may be the only Gospel someone else will ever read." Yet, we cannot give good example to others unless we ourselves are already living out the message clearly in our own lives. This is brought out in another little story involving the holy priest, St. John Marie Vianney, the famous Curé of Ars. There was a young man in France at the time who professed to be an atheist, rejecting all belief in God. He had heard about this zealous priest who heard confessions for many hours each day. He decided, solely out of curiosity, to go to see this famous priest for himself. He was so overwhelmed by his meeting the saintly Curé, that he returned home fervent in his newly re-found faith. An old friend met him some time later and was struck by his evident faith in God. He remarked, "I thought you were an atheist. I thought you did not even believe God exists!" The friend responded: "Oh, I believe God exists all right! I saw Him living in that priest!"

By way of contrast, insincerity and hypocrisy (not living in our daily lives and actions the message we teach others by our words) can be great obstacles to proclaiming the truth effectively. There is another insight that is worth heeding: "I can't hear what you're saying because of what you're doing." Bad example is like "static" that interferes with our transmission of God's truth to others. We need the Holy Spirit to help us live the Truth so that we can proclaim it loud and clear to others, not only by what we say but more importantly by what we do!

REFLECTION QUESTIONS

1. Living the truth means conquering our sinful passions. What are the sinful habits and passions that you struggle with the most? Do you sincerely try to overcome them? What means have you employed to conquer them?

2. Which of the most common rationalizations for persisting in sin do you fall into the most? For example: 1) "Today, everybody is doing it", 2) "The times have changed", 3) "God understands", 4) Anything else?

3. Do you ever resort to denying the wrong you have done or blame others for your wrongdoing? When was the last time you tried to justify the wrong that you did instead of changing your sinful conduct to conform to God's commandments?

4. Are you more attracted to material things or to spiritual things? How might you acquire a more spiritual way of thinking?

5. St. Teresa of Calcutta once said, "No one can give what they do not live!" Are you sincerely and effectively sharing the truth of the Gospel with others by the way that you live?

*Holy Spirit, inspire us with horror of
  sin.*
*Holy Spirit, come and renew the face of
  the earth.*
Holy Spirit, shed Thy light in our souls.
*Holy Spirit, engrave Thy law in our
  hearts.*
*Holy Spirit, inflame us with the flame of
  Thy love.*
*Holy Spirit, open to us the treasures of
  Thy graces.*

—LITANY OF THE HOLY SPIRIT

CHAPTER 10

THE ADVOCATE EMPOWERS US TO PROCLAIM THE TRUTH

*And let the truth be your delight . . . Proclaim it . . . ,
but with a certain congeniality . . . Preach the Truth
as if you had a million voices. It is silence that kills the
world.*

—St. Catherine of Siena

ONCE WE HAVE DISCERNED the truth and lived the truth, we are ready to proclaim the truth to others. The role of the Spirit of Truth continues to be absolutely essential. He keeps us from error while moving us to spread the message about Jesus to others. St. Paul says as much when he writes to the Corinthians:

> I want you to know that no one speaking under the influence of God's Spirit can ever say, "Cursed be Jesus." And no one can say. "Jesus is Lord" except under the influence of the Holy Spirit. (1 Corinthians 12:3)

This aspect of proclaiming the truth about Jesus and about the Catholic Church occupies a tremendously important place in the life of the Church at this time in her history. It has always been a major mission of the Church from the time when Jesus told His Apostles to preach penance for the remission of sins to all the nations (cf. Luke 24:47) and to be His "witnesses in Jerusalem, throughout Judea and Samaria, yes, even to the ends of the earth" (cf. Acts 1:8). The Church will continue this mission to the very end of time, when Jesus returns at His Second Coming to judge all peoples.

Not only are the pope and the bishops as the successors of St. Peter and the Apostles mandated to carry out this mission, but each Catholic is also called to play his or her part. This is rooted first of all in our Baptism, by which each of us was made a child of God. We have an obligation to know Him and love Him ourselves, and then to make Him known and loved by others. This responsibility was increased significantly, as we have already seen, by the sacrament of Confirmation. When we became adult Christians, we were given almost as an official duty the obligation to share in the Church's mission of spreading and defending the Catholic Faith.

The Call to a "New Evangelization" in the Church Today

Now we must add to this responsibility yet another factor, namely, the call issued by Pope St. John Paul II for a "new evangelization" in the Church. There is no doubt that the Holy Spirit directed him to issue what amounts to a magnificent challenge for a new spiritual crusade to promote the cause of Christ and seek the salvation of souls. He issued the summons as the Third Christian Millennium was about to dawn, a time of extraordinary significance for all of humanity in general, and for the life of the Catholic Church in particular. The words of his call in the encyclical *Redemptoris Missio* resound loud and clear:

> I sense that the moment has come to commit all the Church's energies to a "new evangelization." . . . No believer in Christ, no institution of the Church, can avoid this supreme duty: to proclaim Christ to all peoples!

This "New Evangelization" will entail a renewed proclamation of Christ and His "Good News" for all of mankind. It is, and must be seen to be, a joyous message of salvation to a world that has grown increasingly saddened by its own empty materialism. It is a message of light to a world grown dark from a lack of understanding of the true meaning of life. It is a message of hope to a world trapped in its own fatalistic and pessimistic despair. In the language of Pope St. John Paul II, it must proclaim the "Culture of Life" to a world that increasingly identifies itself with the "Culture of Death"! Only the work of the Holy Spirit can produce the fruit of such a "new evangelization" in the Catholic Church!

The Holy Spirit: The "Principal Agent" of the New Evangelization

Pope St. John Paul II constantly stressed the role of the Holy Spirit in the Church's work of evangelization. For example, he stressed this in his apostolic letter, *Tertio Millennio Adveniente*, in preparing the Church for the Jubilee Year 2000:

> The Church cannot prepare for the new millennium in any other way than in the Holy Spirit. What was accomplished by the power of the Holy Spirit "in the fullness of time" can only through the Spirit's power now emerge from the memory of the Church.
>
> The Spirit, in fact, makes present in the Church of every time and place the unique revelation brought by Christ to humanity, making it alive and active in the soul of each individual . . . (#44)

In our own day, too, the Spirit is the principal agent of the new evangelization. Hence it will be important to gain a renewed appreciation of the Spirit as the One Who builds the Kingdom of God within the course of history and prepares its full manifestation in Jesus Christ, stirring people's hearts and quickening in our world the seeds of the full salvation which will come at the end of time. (#45)

"He Has Spoken through the Prophets . . ."

Now we are ready to look more closely at how the Advocate helps us in our mission of proclaiming the truth about Jesus and His Church. There are many ways we can approach this. One is found in the Nicene Creed which we proclaim every Sunday at Mass. We say of the Holy Spirit that "He has spoken through the prophets." This expresses our awareness that the Holy Spirit inspired and directed, beginning with the Old Testament, the revelation and proclamation of God's message to His People through those we call the "prophets." He continues this work even now through those who share in various ways in the "prophetic" or teaching role of Christ and His Church. First He does this through those designated officially to preach and teach the truths of our Catholic Faith, namely, the pope and the bishops in union with him, who constitute the magisterium or official teaching office of the Church. He also does this, as we have seen, through all the faithful who are called to proclaim the truth of Jesus in various ways. Sometimes it will be by their loving dedication to others, especially those in need; at other times it will be by their sincere Christ-like example of faith and piety; finally but frequently, it will be by their words of sharing and instruction. Our focus here will be on the personal role of the faithful, while the role of the magisterium will have to be treated elsewhere at much greater length. Our approach will be to look at the experience of the "prophets" and draw from it valuable insights into how the Holy Spirit continues to speak through us today.

THE EXAMPLE OF THE "PROPHETS"

In the Old Testament, the image of the "prophet" was the image of someone specially called to proclaim the truth to God's people. We can all learn a great deal by reflecting on their role. Often people restrict the idea of a prophet to the notion of someone who, by God's inspiration, foretold future events and happenings of all kinds, from the birth of a child to the scourges of war and plague. But actually, their main role was to proclaim the truth of God's message to His people. Out of love, God had entered into a covenant with His Chosen People; in turn, they were to remain faithful to Him by carrying out their covenant obligations, especially keeping His commandments. The prophets' missions were especially to remind the people of their covenant responsibilities. The prophets, then, were not just "foretellers" of the future, they were primarily "forthtellers" of truth.

Their position was usually not a very enviable one. They were positioned between God and their fellow Israelites, and they had to be faithful to both. Faithful to God, they had to preach His message to the people, no matter how unpopular it was. They also had to be faithful to their fellow Israelites by truthfully telling them God's message, no matter how unwelcome their words were and no matter how violent the opposition.

Being a prophet, then, was no doubt at times a very stressful task. That is why Jeremiah tried to back out of his call to be a prophet, arguing with God that he was too young for the task, and that he was not very good as a public speaker (cf. Jeremiah 1:6). He knew what awaited him. He even complained to God in some tough language about his prophetic ministry:

> You duped me, O Lord, and I let myself be duped; You were too strong for me and You triumphed. All the day I am an object of laughter; everyone mocks me. Whenever I speak I must cry out, violence and outrage is my message; the Word of the Lord has brought me derision and reproach all the day. I say to myself, I will not mention Him, I will speak in His Name no more. But then it becomes like fire burning in my heart, imprisoned in my bones; I grow weary holding it in; I cannot endure it. (Jeremiah 20:7-9)

The true prophets sought God's honor and the spiritual welfare of His People above every and any personal gain or concern. They were committed to the truth, no matter what this cost them, no matter how unpopular, no matter if they stood all alone. As now Venerable Archbishop Fulton J. Sheen—surely a prophet in our own times—once remarked: "The world does not need a voice that is right when everyone else is right, but a voice that is right even when everyone else is wrong."

The true prophets were such a voice! To be a true prophet today, we ourselves must believe the message we preach and teach to others. I once met a man who told me of an encounter he had with Bishop Sheen in midtown Manhattan in New York City. This man was not a Catholic, though his wife was. He spotted Bishop Sheen walking along Madison Avenue and ran up to him with the question: "Bishop Sheen, what must I do if I want to become a Catholic?" The bishop answered, "Find a good priest and he will instruct you." The bishop then continued on to where he was going. The man told me, however, that Bishop Sheen's answer somewhat confused him because he thought every priest was supposed to be good. He told me he waited nearly four hours for the bishop to return from wherever he had gone. When he saw the bishop again, the man ran up to him. The bishop, recognizing the man, asked if he had been waiting all this time. "Yes, Bishop, because your answer confused me. You told me to find a 'good priest' and he would instruct me. Bishop Sheen, I thought all priests were good." The bishop answered: "Priests are like salesmen; some of them believe in their product."

If we don't believe our own message, nobody else will![1] The Spirit of Truth must first convince us of the message if we want to share it effectively with others. A striking example of this is found in the Ordination Rite of a Deacon. At one point in the ceremony, the ordaining bishop hands the newly ordained deacon the Book of the Gospels with these powerful words: "Receive the Gospel of Christ, Whose herald you now are; believe what you read; preach what you believe; and live what you preach!"

For anyone carrying out his or her "prophetic" role in the Church, from an archbishop preaching in a cathedral to a lay volunteer teaching Bible stories to pre-school youngsters, this personal conviction about the message is essential. This, indeed, was the attitude of the "true prophets."

---

1   I once knew a priest-psychologist who, in a talk to a group of friends said: "Sixty-five percent of what you communicate to another person is communicated in the tone of your voice." In other words, by the sense of conviction and enthusiasm in the tone of one's voice, those who hear will know if that person believes what he or she is telling others.

"True Prophets" versus "False Prophets"

There emerged, however, along with the prophets who were faithful and true, another group who were unfaithful and deceitful. Scripture calls them "false prophets." Let us look at some comparisons between the "true prophets" and the "false prophets."

Comparison of Their Attitudes and Approaches

Unlike the "true prophets," the "false prophets" were not committed to truth. Rather, they were "opportunists." They saw the potential of using preaching and teaching for their own personal gain. They recognized that many people preferred a prophet who told them what they wanted to hear, rather than what they needed to hear. So, closing their hearts to the Spirit of Truth, these false prophets proclaimed what their own heart dictated as expedient. They always spoke an attractive and consoling message, one filled with only "good news," things people wanted to hear. In return, those in control who liked to hear what these false prophets had to say granted them "favors." They were rewarded with wealth and positions of prestige and power.

In contrast, the true prophets usually had to call the people to reform. They often had to threaten divine chastisement. They incurred the wrath of many who resented their message of impending punishment. This in turn subjected the true prophets to rejection and often persecution.

Jeremiah's Experience

Jeremiah's prophetic message was a warning to the king and the people that, because of their idolatry and other sins of unfaithfulness against the covenant, God would punish the nation by a humiliating defeat at the hands of a powerful Babylonian army unless they did penance. The false prophets of his day, on the other hand, lulled the people into neglect of their covenant obligations by preaching instead a message of false security. They insisted that the people had a sure sign they would never be defeated because they had the Temple of God in their midst. This turned the hearts of the people against Jeremiah, making them ignore his warnings and even resenting him. This "comforting message" of the false prophets was all an illusion. However, because it was so appealing, it turned out to be a message the people could not reject or maybe simply did not want to reject. Jeremiah's response to the false prophets, however, did not mince a word. He told it "just like it is":

> The following message came to Jeremiah from the Lord: Stand at the gate of the house of the Lord and there proclaim this message: Hear the Word of the Lord, all you of Judah who enter these gates to worship the Lord! Thus says the Lord of hosts; the God of Israel: Reform your ways and your deeds, so that I may remain with you in this place. Put not your trust in the deceitful words: "This is the temple of the Lord! The temple of the Lord! The temple of the Lord!" Only if you thoroughly reform your ways and your deeds; if each of you deals justly with his neighbor; if you no longer oppress the resident

alien, the orphan, and the widow; if you no longer shed innocent blood in this place or follow strange gods to your own harm, will I remain with you in this place, in the land which I gave your fathers long ago and forever. (Jeremiah 7:1-7)

COMPARISON OF THEIR POPULARITY

The true prophets were usually very few in number. Our Lord once told His disciples that they were a "little flock" (Luke 12:32), but He also told them not to be afraid by their minority status. Take the example of the great prophet Elijah. He once stood alone, as God's true prophet, against 450 false prophets of the pagan god, Baal. He won the challenge on the truth of his message. The God of Israel, and not the pagan god Baal, showed Himself to be the true God. In the end, truth always wins out over falsehood.

Even in the New Testament the difference between true prophets and false ones is stressed. We see this in Our Lord's blessings and woes as recorded in the Gospel of St. Luke. First, He tells His disciples that blessings will come to them when they suffer reproach for the sake of the truth, just as the true prophets did:

Blessed are you when men hate you and exclude you and insult you and reject your name as evil on account of the Son of Man. Rejoice on that day and leap for joy, for your reward will be great in heaven; for their fathers treated the prophets in just the same way. (Luke 6:22-23)

On the other hand, He speaks His "woe" to those who, not holding to truth but catering to the people's likes and dislikes, were "popular" like the false prophets.

> Woe to you when all speak well of you. Their fathers treated the false prophets in just this way. (Luke 6:26)

The "true prophets" often lacked a wide popular appeal. The world never gave them a colorful "media" image. Their credibility was questioned; their message was rejected as unacceptable, as old fashioned and "out of touch with reality."

However, there certainly have been exceptions.[2] Despite their minority status and their call for a reformation of life, some of the "true prophets" did enjoy great popularity. There were times they had the support of the "silent majority." St. Anthony of Padua, for example, was immensely popular

---

2 Closer to our own day, who could doubt the popularity of now Venerable Archbishop Fulton J. Sheen? I remember a situation that occurred in a parish where I assisted on certain weekends. After Bishop Sheen had retired, one of the associate parish priests invited the bishop to come for a talk in the parish. The pastor asked the associate if they could possibly fill the 800 seats in the grammar school auditorium? As it turned out, there were so many requests for tickets that they had to rent the local public high school auditorium, which held 1500, and they still had to turn many others away for lack of space.

I also remember another situation involving Bishop Sheen at a local area clergy day of recollection. I had been on it once when less than ten priests participated. On the occasion when Bishop Sheen came to give a similar area clergy recollection day, over 250 priests showed up. Proverbially, they came out of the woodwork to hear him! There was power and charm in his words that attracted people. But he was also very honest and he risked unpopularity with certain groups of people for the sake of preaching the truth.

as a preacher. Blessed as an extraordinary miracle worker, he traveled about northern Italy and southern France, speaking to huge crowds—sometimes throngs of 30,000 or more—which gathered spontaneously whenever they heard he was in the vicinity. Shopkeepers closed their businesses; farmers would come in from the fields. The learned and the illiterate, noblemen and peasants alike came to hear him. Yet, even he had moments when he was ridiculed, held in contempt, publicly challenged, debated, and even rejected. Despite these difficulties, he fearlessly spoke the truth to all, even once openly correcting an archbishop who had been living in a publicly scandalous situation. St. Anthony, the greatest preacher of the Franciscan Order, was both popular and truthful. For "true prophets" like St. Anthony, however, preaching was never—and still today is never—a popularity contest.

False prophets, on the other hand, often thrived on "numbers" of people on their side. They usually enjoyed a favorable image and widespread publicity. For a while, they occupied center stage. This is still true today of many dissident theologians and protesting Catholic clergy or religious. Instant popularity! They may even experience a feeling of being needed, a feeling of having to fight for a cause![3] But when the dissident theologian is silenced, or the protesting priest or religious leaves—in other words, when their "consecrated

---

3   The "false prophets" are allied to the "world," and the world will use them to try to destroy the Church or at least hinder her mission, just as the Jewish authorities used Judas' services to accomplish the capture of Christ. When he went to them afterward with regret and remorse for what he had done, they no longer needed him because he could no longer be of service to them. They told him to take care of his own problems.

state" no longer exists—it is not surprising or uncommon that the popularity vanishes. Such persons suddenly find themselves without the "status" they once seemed to have had such a tight hold on; but even more sadly, they usually find themselves estranged from the Church they once loved!

COMPARISON OF THEIR MESSAGE

Truth Endures, Falsehood Passes Away

The message of the true prophet has endured and continues to endure because all truth is rooted in God Himself Who is Eternal Truth. His predictions are always fulfilled. His promises never fail. As God will be forever, so will His Word endure forever! Our Lord Himself said of His own teaching, that even though all of creation as we know it will pass away, His teaching will stand forever:

> The heavens and the earth will pass away, but My words will not pass away. (Mark 13:31)

The message of the false prophet, however, is accepted only for a time. When its empty promises fail, and its deceitful expectations are recognized for what they really are, the message of the false prophet quickly passes away.[4] In the end, it has nothing secure in which to root itself.

---

4   Many people were deceived by the false expectations of Communism, and were lured for a time by it. But when they experienced its true nature as a godless, oppressive, totalitarian political system, they quickly became disillusioned with it. As one former ardent communist turned ardent anti-communist put it: "If you are twenty years old and you are not a communist, you are crazy; and if you are forty years old and you are still a communist, you are crazy."

Two Important
Effects of Proclaiming
the Truth Faithfully

Truth Consoles and Challenges

When we preach the message of truth—after first believing it and living it ourselves—it strengthens and consoles those who want to hear it. Good people receive great moral support and encouragement when they hear the teachings of Christ and the Church proclaimed strongly and clearly from the pulpit and in the classroom. On the other hand, those who resist the message of truth often are upset by what they hear.

Dorothy Day, a former Communist Party member who later converted to Catholicism, used to say: "Jesus came for two reasons—to comfort the afflicted and to afflict the comfortable." If the message is strong enough and clear enough it may well upset some people, but at the same time it may also move some of these same people to reflect once again on their own position or point of view. If, on the other hand, the message is too bland or watered down, it most likely won't upset anybody, but it probably won't get anybody thinking either. I believe a lot of our youth have left the Church, not because the teaching of the Church was "too strict" or "out of touch with the times." Rather, I believe it was often toned down so much in an effort not to offend the young that the message no longer had any appeal left to attract them. All the challenge was taken out of it. Rather than presenting the Gospel in such a way that it challenges our young people to

173

change their lives[5] (which is what conversion is all about), we can be tempted to change the Gospel to make it fit more comfortably with where they are at already, so they do not have to change at all.

Truth Has Power and Authority

The Scriptures say that the people who heard Jesus preach hung onto His every word because He taught with authority and not like the Scribes and Pharisees (cf. Mark 1:22, 27). Now we know today that Jesus' "authority" to teach what He did was rooted in His divinity; but the people who heard Him preach, especially at the beginning of His public ministry, did not know of His divinity or even that He was the promised Messiah. Rather, His "authority" with the crowds came from the power of His own conviction and the sincerity of His life. It was evident that He said what He believed and believed what He said. Even His opponents, despite their

---

5   Someone who really challenged the youth of our day and gave them the whole Gospel message without watering it down was Pope St. John Paul II. Youth the world over loved him, respected him, and flocked to him! I was privileged to be at the World Day of Prayer for Youth in Denver, Colorado in August of 1993. I remember his mass at Cherry Creek Park before a vast throng of young people. At one point after his homily and even after the Creed, he went to the microphone and told the young people he had to correct something he had said in his homily. "I told you not to be ashamed of your Catholic Faith," he said. Then he added: "I have to correct myself. . . . Be proud of your Catholic Faith!" The young people cheered wildly. The truth from him never turned the youth off from the Faith. In fact, it visibly turned them on to Christ and the Church.

frequent deceitfulness, had to admit His honesty and His unwillingness to compromise with human respect:

> Waiting their chance, they (the scribes and chief priests) sent spies who pretended to be upright men so they could seize on what He said in order to hand Him over to the authority and power of the Procurator. And they put this question to Him: "Teacher, we know You speak and teach plainly and without regard for the person; instead, You teach the way of God in truth . . ." (Luke 20:20-21)

Our Lord was "faithful" to the message His Heavenly Father gave Him to preach. We in turn must be faithful to the message He gave us to proclaim in His Name. This is so important that St. Paul lays down "faithfulness" as the first quality of a true servant of the Lord (cf. 1 Corinthians 4:1-2). Let us ask the Holy Spirit to give us the conviction and courage necessary to proclaim the truth faithfully by all we say and do.

If all of us faithfully carry out our mission to proclaim Jesus and His truth anew in our time, under the direction of the Advocate, we will see the wonderful words of Pope St. John Paul II come true:

> If all the sons and daughters of the Church become tireless missionaries of the Gospel, a new flowering of holiness and renewal will spring up in this world!

Reflection Questions

1. Do you accept your duty as a baptized Christian to proclaim Christ to all peoples?

2. How can you distinguish a true prophet from a false prophet?

3. Dorothy Day once said that, "Jesus came for two reasons—to comfort the afflicted and to afflict the comfortable." What does this mean? Do you know of anyone in our day and age who does this for people?

Holy Spirit, teach us to pray well.
Holy Spirit, enlighten us with Thy
heavenly inspirations.
Holy Spirit, lead us in the way of
salvation.
Holy Spirit, grant us the only necessary
knowledge.
Holy Spirit, inspire in us the practice of
good.
Holy Spirit, grant us the merits of all
virtues.

—LITANY OF THE HOLY SPIRIT

CHAPTER 11

THE ADVOCATE STRENGTHENS US TO DEFEND THE TRUTH

This power of the Spirit is more necessary than ever for the Christians of our time who are asked to bear witness to their faith in a world which is often indifferent, if not hostile and deeply marked by relativism and hedonism. It is a power essential to all preachers who must offer the Gospel anew without yielding to compromises and false short-cuts, by proclaiming the truth about Christ "in season and out of season" (2 Timothy 4:2).

—Pope St. John Paul II
General Audience, July 1, 1998

IT HAS BEEN SAID THAT human life on earth is a warfare, a continuous struggle between good and evil. Experience confirms this for us. Like the downward pull of gravity when we try to go upward, evil forces are always attempting to prevent our progress along the journey to eternal life. Fittingly, then, does the Old Testament writer, Ben Sirach, remind us:

> When you come to serve the Lord, prepare your-
> self for trials. Be sincere of heart and steadfast . . .
> Cling to Him, forsake Him not . . . for in fire
> gold is tested and worthy men in the crucible of
> humiliation. Trust God and He will help you . . .
> (Sirach 2:1-2, 5-6)

Now this struggle is a reality not only in our personal lives, but in the very communal life of the Church itself. It is seen throughout the whole history of the Church. And much of this struggle, especially when it comes from within, is the struggle to preserve and defend truth in the Church and in human society, the truth of God's Revelation to all mankind centering on the Person of Jesus Our Lord, and flowing from His teachings. From the fall of our first parents, Adam and Eve, by the Original Sin which introduced untruth into God's creation, down to this present day and lasting until the very end of time, this struggle to preserve and defend the truth has and will continue to be a very real part of our human existence!

This must make us vigilant. Vigilance or caution is required if we are to preserve and defend the truth. The reason is that evil often tries to promote itself under the appearance of something good. That is the way false prophets operate: trying to make us think that evil is good and that good is evil. Our Lord Himself compared "false prophets" to wolves on the prowl who come hidden underneath sheep's clothing (cf. Matthew 7:15). Their appearance allows them to come unsus-pected and undetected until they are close enough to attack the flock and do it great harm. Naivete about the presence and power of evil is not a Christian virtue! In important matters, it can allow serious harm to happen in the Church.

There are many ways in which truth can be attacked. We have already seen some of these in previous chapters. Here, let us focus on two specific temptations against truth. The first is the temptation to distort the truth on the part of some within the Church who no longer hold to sound, orthodox teaching. The second is the temptation that often faces those who believe the truth to be pressured into compromising it.

Resisting the Temptation to Distort the Truth

St. Paul's Struggles to Defend the Faith

St. Paul was certainly aware of the need for vigilance. He had been the Lord's instrument to plant the Church in many communities in ancient Asia Minor (modern-day Turkey) and Greece. He had no illusions that once these local Church communities were established, everything would run smoothly. Like a watchful mother, he was truly vigilant—always alert for trouble, especially from within the community. This is why he puts at the end of his stirring list of sufferings for the sake of Jesus and the preaching of the Gospel his tremendous concern for the various Church communities:

> Leaving other sufferings unmentioned, there is
> that daily tension pressing on me, my anxiety for
> all the churches. (2 Corinthians 11:28)

Corinth: Evidence of St. Paul's Vigilance

Trouble from outside the community, such as persecution, is more obvious, and could be more easily recognized and opposed. This is not the case with trouble from within the community. St. Paul feared, for example, that his converts at Corinth, lacking adequate vigilance, would easily be led astray from the truth into various distortions by insincere and trouble-making members of the community there:

> I wish that you would bear with me in a little foolishness. Put up with me, I beg you! For I am jealous for you with the jealousy of God Himself, because I betrothed you like a pure virgin to be presented to one husband—to Christ. But I am afraid that just as the serpent deceived Eve with his cunning, your minds will somehow be led away from a sincere devotion to Christ. For if someone comes and proclaims a different Jesus than we proclaimed, or if you receive a different spirit than the One you received from us, or a gospel other than the Gospel you received from us, you seem to bear it quite readily. (2 Corinthians 11:1-4)

And there were plenty of troublemakers stirring things up in the Church in Corinth. St. Paul, who also lists being endangered by "false brothers" as one of the significant crosses in his life (cf. 2 Corinthians 11:26), knew the need to safeguard the truth at Corinth only too well. He had to oppose those whom he described as "super apostles," who were interfering in the Church community there and stirring up dissension by their false teachings. He actually called them "false apostles" who practiced the deceit of Satan—whom they were really serving—despite trying to pass themselves off as servants of Christ.

> Such men are false apostles, dishonest workers who disguise themselves as apostles of Christ. There is nothing remarkable in this; after all, even Satan disguises himself as an angel of light. So it should come as no surprise if Satan's servants disguise themselves as ministers of righteousness. But their end will correspond to their deeds. (2 Corinthians 11:13-15)

St. Paul was on guard to save the Church in Corinth for Jesus. Despite the temporary disruption, the Corinthians eventually held firmly to the truth. However, in other circumstances, the outcome for St. Paul was not always this successful.

Galatia: Anguish to the Heart of St. Paul

Another example of St. Paul's vigilance was for his Galatian converts. His letter to them reflects the fact that the greatest apostolic pain and disappointment he suffered was in connection with the Church in Galatia. A group of hard-line Jewish "converts" to Christianity, still holding rigidly to circumcision and to all the dietary and other prescriptions of the Mosaic law, were stirring up trouble within the various communities that St. Paul had founded. They were demanding that every Gentile convert to Christianity had to observe all the prescriptions of the Old Testament. These agitators were known as the "Judaizers." Their teaching in effect denied the need for faith in Christ for salvation. Unfortunately, they enjoyed great success in Galatia, drawing many in the community away from St. Paul's solid teaching. In response to the situation. the Apostle addressed some sharp words to the Church in Galatia:

> I am amazed that you are so quick to desert the One Who called you by the grace of Christ, and are turning to another gospel. There is no other gospel, of course, but there are some who are disturbing you and trying to distort the Gospel of Christ. But even if we, or an angel from Heaven, should proclaim to you a gospel not in accord with the one we delivered to you, let him be accursed! (Galatians 1:6-8)

St. Paul is stressing the point here that there is only one Gospel, one message of salvation revealed by God. If there were a "second" gospel, it would mean either that God has revealed something new that contradicted what He revealed originally, or else that God did not reveal it and so it is nothing but a fabrication by those who falsely speak in His name.

THE EXPERIENCE OF THE "APOLOGISTS"

Throughout the long history of the Catholic Church, God has raised up great defenders of the Faith. Significant among these was a group in the early Church called the "Apologists."

They played a prominent role during the persecutions of the Church in the ancient Roman Empire.

> The Apologists take their name from the Greek word *apologia*, which means "defense." They took up the pen to defend the new Christian religion from the accusations and attacks of the surrounding pagan society. They were able to carry out this defense with all the more success inasmuch as they were themselves almost always converts from paganism. By defending their new religious confession, the Apologists, pagan intellectuals who had converted to Christianity, intended at the same time to justify their own conversion to themselves and others and to offer adequate and cogent reasons for it on the plane of moral choice and philosophical research. But why, one may ask, was it necessary to defend Christianity and from what specific accusations? (*Introduction to the Fathers of the Church*, Edizioni Instituto San Gaetano, Vicenza, Italy, 1982, p. 49).

What accusations were being leveled against the early Christians? Some accusations came from the common people and were more in the nature of popular prejudices and suspicions in the face of the little known and greatly misunderstood teachings and practices of the Christians. Some of these accusations were: (1) cannibalism: due to a misunderstanding of the doctrine on the Holy Eucharist, the early Christians were accused of feeding on the flesh of a child;

(2) incest: the obvious reciprocal love between brothers and sisters was sometimes misrepresented as sexual; and (3) atheism: because the Christians totally disregarded the gods of the traditional pagan religion. This attitude was further exaggerated to appear like a threat to the political stability and economic prosperity of the Empire. Such popular prejudices, along with the fear and distrust of anything new, often gave rise to a flood of persecution and alienation.

Other accusations were more sophisticated, being of an intellectual and philosophical nature. These were considered more dangerous, and so required a more intellectual response. Christians were accused of: (1) drawing their members from the socially inferior classes, such as despised manual workers and "blue collar" trades as well as credulous women, children, and slaves; (2) rejecting the pagan ideals in matters of philosophy and wealth, and even maintaining that Christian women and children could have a wisdom greater than their pagan husbands and fathers; (3) disregarding the welfare of the Roman Empire by shunning involvement in politics and rejecting military service; and (4) teaching unreasonable doctrine, such as the Incarnation, because they considered the notion that God became a little child as utter nonsense.

> In the face of these attacks, Christians wanted to enlighten public opinion and defend themselves. In their writings they tried to give a clear presentation of their beliefs and practices in order to put an end to misunderstandings. These writings were called "apologies," a term

indicating defense or justification... They wrote for those who did not share their faith—the emperor, magistrates, the intelligentsia, public opinion. They had to work out a language intelligible to those for whom they were writing, that is to say, in terms of Graeco-Latin culture. In this way, Christianity broke free from its cultural isolation. The apologists Hellenized Christianity and Christianized Hellenism. In this way they worked out a first theology... All the apologists pointed out the injustice of the accusations against the Christians, the judgments and condemnations at the time of the persecutions. They demolished one by one the charges made against them (Jean Comby, *How to Read Church History*, Crossroad Publishing Co., New York, 1990, pp. 33-34)

Our Need for Watchfulness in the Church Today

St. Paul as well as the Apologists knew that vigilance was needed by the community as well as by each individual so that no evil influence would enter. I remember reading in the writings of one of the early Desert Fathers that all that is needed for sin to grow in strength within a person's heart is for just one evil thought to take root in it. Such an entrenched evil thought will gradually spread like a malignant cancer, bringing the destruction of all virtue and goodness in its wake. What can happen to an individual can similarly happen to a local church community.

By our Baptism, we have been given new life in Christ. We have also become sons and daughters of the Church. This should move us to be not only loyal to the Church's beliefs ourselves, but to be ready to defend those beliefs when they are criticized, distorted or rejected by others. Even more, as we saw previously, by the sacrament of Confirmation we are called to be courageous witnesses of Christ, witnessing to His truths given to us in and by the Catholic Church. As we have already seen, before the changes after Vatican Council II in the Rite of Confirmation, the bishop would give a light slap on the cheek to each person he confirmed. It was a reminder to be ready to suffer to defend our Catholic Faith. We were told to be "adult Christians" and "soldiers of Jesus Christ." We must all do this according to our responsibilities in the Church as well as the gifts of grace and the training in the Faith we have received, whether one be a bishop, a priest, a deacon, a religious, a married or single lay person in whatever capacity. We should each do what we can to defend the teachings of the Church. What would be worst of all would be to remain silent in the face of verbal attacks on the Faith. As an old saying puts it: "All that is needed for evil (like distortions of truth) to succeed is for good people to do or say nothing!"

RESISTING THE TEMPTATION TO COMPROMISE THE TRUTH

St. Paul cautioned that people can be tempted to present their own version of the "good news," which would really be "bad news" for anyone who believes in it and trusts in it for their salvation. People can especially be tempted to present as God's message what they really know will be popular with their listeners. St. Paul was very aware that the "false apostles" catered to popularity. Man of honesty and principle that he was, he only spoke the truth, no matter what its popularity rating. That is why he adds regarding the Gospel as he preached it:

> Whom would you say I am trying to please at this point—men or God? Is this how I seek to ingratiate myself with men? If I were trying to win men's approval. I would surely not be serving Christ! (Galatians 1:10)

It can be a great temptation for those who preach and teach to compromise their message or alter it simply to satisfy people. A little cartoon I ran across some years ago expressed this well. It showed two preachers in a sacristy room looking at a collection basket that had no dollar bills in it, only a few coins. Through the open doorway one could see some stern faces on people in the congregation. One preacher was talking to the other. The caption underneath the cartoon read: "I think we had better go back to preaching those vague generalities!"

The Moment of Truth

I believe that every preacher and teacher at some point in their ministry, and probably every one of the faithful at some point in their lives, will have to face their "moment of truth" when a situation or temptation to compromise the Gospel message will confront them. Do I follow my conscience, or do I follow the crowd? Do I say what I believe in my heart, or do I say what I think others want to hear me say?

I would like to share such a situation that occurred in my life, one that I have long felt confronted me with this question. I was teaching religion in a Catholic high school at the time. My course was one on marriage and sexual morality. One day, quite unexpectedly, another priest on the faculty said to me: "You're too direct with the students. You're going to drive them away!" I understood immediately what he was telling me: "Tone it down! Bend the rules a little! Don't make it black and white—use a lot of gray!"

I felt myself facing a crucial decision in my life. What was I to do? The other priest had just gotten his degree in religious studies—was he right about the "new morality" so current then? I did not agree. After all, the Ten Commandments were from God, and He did not change them, so how could I? Furthermore, I began to reflect on the priest's other statement that I would "drive the students away"! As I thought about it, I disagreed. I felt that being "popular" with the students was not my purpose in teaching them. I also never expected that all the students would agree with everything that I taught about sexuality and morality. Even Our Lord Himself did not please everybody who heard Him preach. At the same time, I knew I could not teach them something which I did not believe. I was convinced that I would have to render an account to God on the Day of Judgment for my teaching. In the process, if I had misled any students into sin by false teaching, I knew that I would be held accountable before the Lord.

I was convinced, therefore, that before I would ever teach my students something I knew to be wrong, it would be better for me to give up teaching. At the same time, I felt that, unlike popularity, if I honestly taught the students what I really believed (and knew) was correct, they would respect me for it. I also realized that for those who sincerely wanted to live by true Catholic morality, my teaching would strengthen and encourage their convictions. Even for those students who would be "upset" by my holding to the moral teachings of the Catholic Church and who might not be ready to live them out at this time in their lives, I felt that my honest teachings, maybe years later, might influence their lives. (After all, even the great St. Augustine had struggled for twelve years in his adolescence and young adult life to gain chastity, despite all that his saintly mother Monica had taught him.)

So I stood my ground. If they would have asked me to leave the faculty, that would have been their decision; but I knew what my own decision had to be. I chose to be faithful to authentic Catholic moral teaching! I have often thought back on this situation and wondered, as a result of subsequent events, whether the priest's remark may not have expressed some personal confusion he himself was experiencing at that time in his own life. I do not think he ever realized the crisis of conscience his remark brought upon me. But in many ways, I have come to see that this trial helped me to clarify my own ministry and the need to choose to be faithful in teaching the truths of the Catholic Church to others.

Truth and Love Go Together

Defending the Truth "in Love"

Preachers and teachers need the Spirit of Truth to help them not only to know the truth from its counterfeits, but to grow in their conviction to uphold the truth, and then to preach and teach the truth with love, as St. Paul admonishes us (cf. Ephesians 4:15). The faithful must do the same in their own set of circumstances. Truth and love must go together. Truth without love can be dry and unattractive. It can even be made to appear as harsh or abrasive, and therefore repulsive. Love in the manner and motive of sharing the truth with others can make it very appealing to sincere, open-minded, and open-hearted people. Love without truth, on the other side of the coin, lacks a necessary solidness. It would be comparable to the human body without a skeleton, a shapeless blob! It would be superficial and mediocre at best, all fluff at worst! As such, it would lack the driving force needed to lead us to a deeper union with Christ. It would indeed be to build on sand and not on a solid rock foundation! We must faithfully convey Christ's message because we are His servants and have been entrusted by Him with this ministry. At the same time we should present the truth with understanding and compassion for people's weaknesses and their need to mature in the truth. We must always be aware of their struggles and of the possibility that they may fail in their efforts from time to time, just as we who preach and teach also fail! After all, we must practice what we preach.

Defending the Truth "Out of Love"

We should fulfill our ministry out of dedicated loving concern for the spiritual welfare of our brothers and sisters in Christ. Even if and when we ourselves fall short of living as we should, we must still remain faithful to proclaiming the truth to others. We do this just as we would want someone else to preach and teach the truth to us when we most need to hear it. In the Scriptures, St. Paul tells us we must proclaim the truth openly; those who are of sincere heart will accept it:

> Since we received this ministry through God's mercy, we do not lose heart. Rather, we renounce shameful deeds done in secret, refusing to employ deceit or to water down the word of God. Instead, by openly proclaiming the truth, we commend ourselves to the conscience of all men in the sight of God. (2 Corinthians 4:1-2)

THE SPIRIT OF TRUTH
DEFENDS US BY HIS WISDOM

We need the Spirit of Truth because He safeguards the truths that have been revealed to us. First, He gives witness to our own human spirit of what is truth. Then He strengthens us to remain firm in our allegiance to the truth. Finally, He gives us the words of wisdom we need to speak the truth as we witness to others and to defend it when called upon to do so.

The Moment of Trust

If facing the temptation to compromise the truth instead of defending it wholeheartedly can be called "the moment of truth," then the trial of believing whether the Holy Spirit will assist us or not when we are put on the spot for our Catholic Faith can rightly be called "the moment of trust."

I remember an interesting story that illustrates this point very well. It involved an Italian missionary to China in the 1940s named Archbishop Polio. He related the story himself to a group of seminarians I was with. He told us he was at one time the youngest archbishop in the world, as well as the spiritual head of one of the largest archdioceses in the world, consisting of a huge section of southern China. He had been expelled from China when the Communists took over around 1950. But before he was expelled, he was put on trial by the Communists. All during his trial period, he remembered Our Lord's words:

> Behold, I am sending you out like sheep among wolves. Be as wise as serpents and as guileless as doves. But be on your guard with respect to men. They will hale you into court, they will flog you in their synagogues. You will be brought to trial before rulers and kings, to give witness before them and before the Gentiles on My account. When they hand you over, do not worry about what you will say or how you will say it. When the hour comes, you will be given what you are to say. You yourselves will not be the speakers; the Spirit

of your Father will be speaking in you. (Matthew 10:16-20)

The trial was conducted in such a way that the archbishop was daily brought into a courtroom packed with people for purposes of propaganda. The Communists wanted to make a spectacle of him, accusing him of collaborating secretly with many "capitalist" countries that were really enemies of the people of China. By doing this, the Communists hoped to discredit the Catholic Church in the eyes of the Chinese people. During the period of the trial, a young Communist lawyer routinely held up papers so that everyone in the courtroom could see them. He said that these papers were letters the archbishop had received from various "capitalist countries," and they indicated that he was a spy working in league with these foreign countries to betray the people of China. The young communist lawyer said he had found these letters in the archbishop's own office at his residence.

All through the trial, the archbishop remained calm, trusting that the Holy Spirit would give him the words to say in his own defense. Finally, after many accusations had been made against him and the trial had gone on for weeks, the archbishop was asked if he had anything to say in his own defense. He said, "Yes, I want to ask a question of the lawyer who has accused me of these things." Now the archbishop had told us that in China, the norm of whether a person is considered sane or not is whether they know their right from their left. If they know their right from their left, they are considered mentally competent. If they do not, they are considered mentally incompetent. The archbishop challenged the young lawyer, "You said you found these letters in my office at my episcopal residence. On what side of the stairs is my office located in my residence, on the right or on the left?" The lawyer, of course, had made up all these charges against the archbishop. He had never been to the archbishop's residence; and so he had no idea where the office was located in his residence. But since everyone in the courtroom was waiting for an answer, the young lawyer had to say something. Finally he said, "Of course, your office is on the right side of the stairs." The archbishop said, "No, my office is located on the left side of the stairs. Now, if you can't tell your right from your left, how can you accuse me of all these things?" Everyone in the courtroom burst into laughter! That young Communist lawyer was completely discredited. In fact, the archbishop told us the young lawyer never returned to the courtroom to continue the case.

The Spirit of Truth had truly given the archbishop wisdom which his adversary was not able to overcome. This same Spirit of Truth is, indeed, the Advocate, always at our side giving us a strong defense, and when we need it, a strong offense in the cause of defending and proclaiming the truth.

Come, Advocate, Spirit of Truth

From all that has been written in this book—and it only scratches the surface regarding the role of the Spirit of Truth—we can see why Jesus told His Apostles not to go forth from Jerusalem to preach in Judea, Samaria, and even to the ends of the earth until they had first received the Holy Spirit.

He was the fulfillment of the Heavenly Father's promise and the power from on high needed to carry out their mission of worldwide evangelization (cf. Acts 1:4-8).

Today, we need this same Holy Spirit to come to us to help us recall and grasp all that Jesus taught us. We need the Spirit of Truth to confirm us in this truth, and then lead us forth to proclaim Jesus courageously by all we do and say as part of the "new evangelization" we have been called to by Pope St. John Paul II, Pope Benedict XVI, and Pope Francis.

Let us ask Our Blessed Lady, the Spouse of the Holy Spirit, She who was most open to His working in her life, to obtain for us the working of the Spirit of Truth in our own lives.

* * * * *

Holy Spirit, come confirm us
In the truth that Christ makes known;
We have faith and understanding
Through Your helping gifts alone.

Holy Spirit, come, console us,
Come as Advocate to plead,
Loving Spirit from the Father,
Grant in Christ the help we need.

Holy Spirit, come, renew us,
Come Yourself to make us live:
Holy through your loving presence,
Holy through the gifts you give.

Holy Spirit, come, possess us,
You the love of Three in One.
Holy Spirit of the Father,
Holy Spirit of the Son.

(Music by Richard Redhead; 1820–1901:
Text by Brian Foley, as quoted in *The
Liturgy of the Hours*, Vol. 3, Catholic Book
Publishing Co., New York, 1975, p. 661)

Reflection Questions

1. Evil often tries to promote itself in the guise of something good. Can you cite any modern-day examples of messages that the world "twists" in order to promote certain errors?

2. Have you ever experienced a "moment of truth," when a situation or temptation to compromise the gospel message confronted you? If so, what did you do? Did you follow your conscience or did you do or say what you thought others wanted you to do or say?

3. Why is it essential always to preach the truth in love?

*Grant, O merciful Father, that Thy
Divine Spirit may enlighten, inflame,
and purify us, that He may penetrate
us with His heavenly dew and make us
fruitful in good works, through Our Lord
Jesus Christ, Thy Son, Who with Thee,
in the unity of the same Spirit, lives and
reigns forever and ever. Amen.*

—LITANY OF THE HOLY SPIRIT

TAN·BOOKS

TAN Books is the Publisher You Can Trust With Your Faith.

TAN Books was founded in 1967 to preserve the spiritual, intellectual, and liturgical traditions of the Catholic Church. At a critical moment in history TAN kept alive the great classics of the Faith and drew many to the Church. In 2008 TAN was acquired by Saint Benedict Press. Today TAN continues to teach and defend the Faith to a new generation of readers.

TAN publishes more than 600 booklets, Bibles, and books. Popular subject areas include theology and doctrine, prayer and the supernatural, history, biography, and the lives of the saints. TAN's line of educational and homeschooling resources is featured at TANHomeschool.com.

TAN publishes under several imprints, including TAN, Neumann Press, ACS Books, and the Confraternity of the Precious Blood. Sister imprints include Saint Benedict Press, Catholic Courses, and Catholic Scripture Study.

For more information about TAN,
or to request a free catalog, visit
TANBooks.com

Or call us toll-free at
(800) 437-5876

TAN · CLASSICS

A collection of the finest literature
in the Catholic tradition.

978-0-89555-227-3   978-0-89555-154-2   978-0-89555-155-9

Our TAN Classics collection is a well-balanced sampling
of the finest literature in the Catholic tradition.

978-0-89555-230-3   978-0-89555-228-0   978-0-89555-151-1

TAN · BOOKS

978-0-89555-153-5

978-0-89555-149-8

978-0-89555-199-3

The collection includes distinguished spiritual works of
the saints, philosophical treatises and famous biographies.

978-0-89555-226-6

978-0-89555-152-8

978-0-89555-225-9

Visit us at TANBooks.com

Spread the Faith with . . .

TAN·BOOKS

A Division of Saint Benedict Press, LLC

TAN books are powerful tools for evangelization. They lift the mind to God and change lives. Millions of readers have found in TAN books and booklets an effective way to teach and defend the Faith, soften hearts, and grow in prayer and holiness of life.

Throughout history the faithful have distributed Catholic literature and sacramentals to save souls. St. Francis de Sales passed out his own pamphlets to win back those who had abandoned the Faith. Countless others have distributed the Miraculous Medal to prompt conversions and inspire deeper devotion to God. Our customers use TAN books in that same spirit.

If you have been helped by this or another TAN title, share it with others. Become a TAN Missionary and share our life changing books and booklets with your family, friends and community. We'll help by providing special discounts for books and booklets purchased in quantity for purposes of evangelization. Write or call us for additional details.

TAN Books
Attn: TAN Missionaries Department
PO Box 410487
Charlotte, NC 28241

Toll-free (800) 437-5876
missionaries@TANBooks.com